Simple Scrapbooks

Ideas and Techniques

Joshua
Alec
COLD LIPS WARM HEARTS
Take 2 kids, 2 inches of snow, a little imagination and a whole lot of love. add it all together and end up with a memory that Mommy will cherish for a lifetime.
Nov. 2002

Simple Scrapbooks™

Ideas and Techniques

The Editors of Simple Scrapbooks magazine

Hugh Lauter Levin Associates, Inc.

ISBN: 0-88363-942-4

Project Director: Leslie Conron Carola
Design: Kathleen Herlihy-Paoli
Editor: Deborah Cannarella

The scrapbook page ideas featured are from the readers and artists of *Simple Scrapbooks* magazine.
www.simplescrapbooksmag.com

Printed in Hong Kong

Cookie Love
Savannah Claire

ALL STAR KIDS

infinite
Possibility

Jemma's

CONTENTS

Yankee Doodle
Daniel
July 4, 2001

Introduction

I'd hate for people to miss out on the amazing experience of creating a scrapbook—because they think it will take too much time, money, or creativity. You don't have to be artistic to scrapbook. You don't even have to like "crafts." You don't have to have a stockpile of paper and stickers and all the latest doodads. And you definitely don't have to give up all your free time. The only thing you really need is you—busy, overworked, under-organized you. With your unique perspective on life, and a few photographs, you can be well on your way to beautiful, meaningful scrapbooks! You Can Scrapbook. *Simple Scrapbooks: Ideas and Techniques* and *Simple Scrapbooks* magazine is on a mission to prove it to you.

The philosophies that guide our magazine content were born out of necessity. I started scrapbooking over ten years ago, after my first child was born. I jumped in feet-first and went absolutely hog wild. I took pictures, made pages, took more pictures and made more pages. I scrapbooked everything from excursions to the park to trips to the dentist. I took the neighbor kids for ice cream one day, so I could construct an ice-cream page that I had dreamt about the night before.

I would have continued merrily along in my newfound hobby, except that life got in the way and baby #2 was born. I started to fall behind, way behind. As the pictures stacked up, I began to feel overwhelmed and uninspired. What had been a creative outlet became a chore—and I didn't need another chore. And then baby #3 was born. Like many people who avoid scrapbooking, whether they've tried it or not, I assumed I had to work in chronological order and stay current with all of my pictures. NOT TRUE!

◀ **FREEDOM,** *by Kim Heffington, Avondale, AZ. One great photograph and one repeated stamp image on a one color background, all as charming as the subject herself. This certainly captures the idea of simple scrapbooking.*

◀◀ **YANKEE DOODLE DANIEL,** *by Kim Heffington, Avondale, AZ. A handsome young boy—barefoot, smiling, and waving a flag—is the epitome of an American 4th of July. Who could resist scrapbooking this joy?*

Fast forward to 2004. I take more pictures now than ever. The difference is I don't let them drive my scrapbooking. I've learned there is a difference between scrapbooking your pictures and scrapbooking your memories. These days I slip most of my photos into photo albums, where they can be immediately enjoyed, and I save the best of the best to scrapbook. Rather than spending my limited time on one ongoing family album, I've decided to create smaller projects that focus on the people who matter most to me, and the influence they've had on my life. Here's what I've done so far:

- A small accordion album that highlights the life of my mother-in-law, Valerie. Valerie passed away several years ago, and this project has given me a reason to get my husband talking about his memories. I now have something tangible to use in teaching my children more about her.

- An 8 x 8 album entitled "My Boys," wherein I've combined photos and journaling to "freeze" in time each of my four boys and their strikingly different personalities. No matter how fast they grow up, I have a place I can turn to "go back in time."

A super simple "Girls Weekend" binder that gathers together the wisdom and wit shared at our annual mom-and-daughters retreat. Did you know that a plastic knife cuts through hot brownies like butter!

- A non-traditional album, housed in a DVD case, for Simple Scrapbooks Creative Editor and cohort Wendy Smedley. Working together, we've become the dearest of friends, the kind that finish each other's sentences. I wanted her to know how much she means to me.

- A fun little metal book called "My Life, 2004." I started with an ABC list of 26 words that describe my life right now: A is for abundant, B is for busy, C is for cluttered, etc. I've gathered photos to illustrate these words and used one coordinated product line to pull it all together. Of all the people you choose to scrapbook, you are the most important. There is just one story you are truly qualified to tell—your own. If you're not doing it, who else will?

The year's not over yet, and I have a few more projects up my sleeve. What I want you to realize

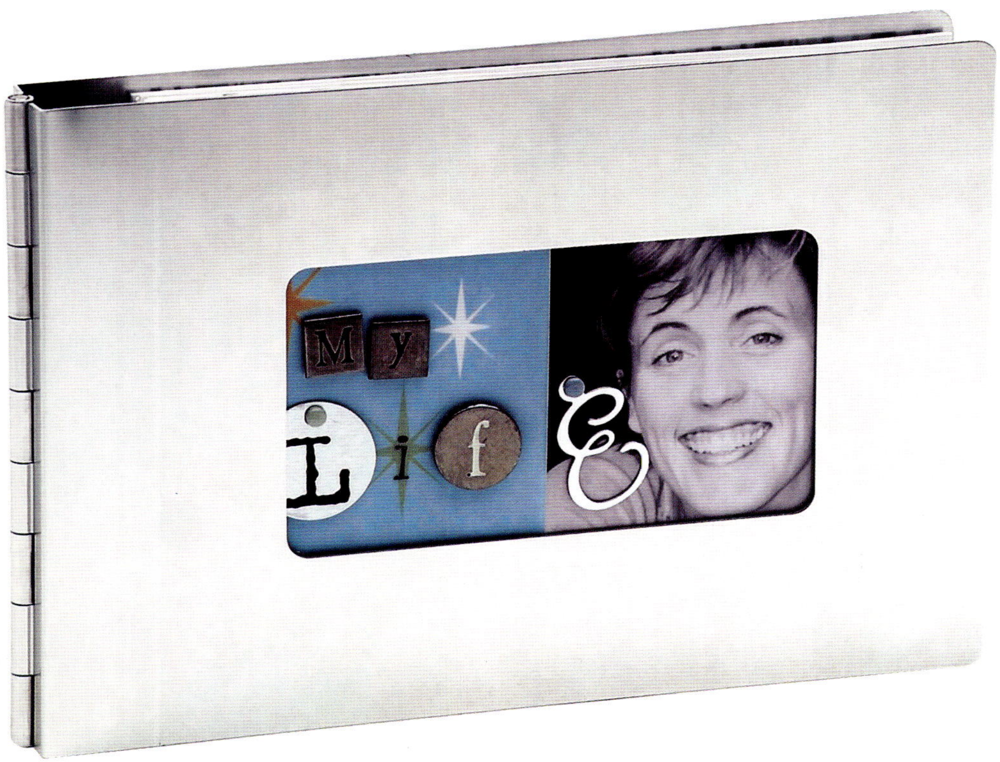

My Life, 2004, *by Stacy Julian, Liberty Lake, WA. An elegant little metal book with this year's memories. A scrapbooking project to start and finish with ease.*

is that I am scrapbooking my family's life. No, you won't find a complete record detailing what happened during each month. What you will find are real-life glimpses into who we are and what is important to us. What the Simple Scrapbooks project approach might lack in accuracy, it makes up in authenticity and meaning. Learn more about compiling such theme albums in chapter one.

Approach is one thing, the confidence to create is quite another. At *Simple Scrapbooks* magazine we emphasize the fundamentals of photography, writing, color, and design so that you can become a stronger scrapbooker. As you learn to apply time-honored principles, your creative intuition grows and your tendency to second-guess yourself diminishes. Then you get more done in less time, and the end-result is far more pleasing.

You're going to love the scrapbook pages in this book. They are presented in chapters dedicated to these fundamentals (see chapters 2 through 5), and every layout shares a tip, trick, or technique—so you take away far more than just a page idea. You can start your "low-key" schooling right here with the pages in this introduction! When you discover a design that you are really drawn to, take a moment to evaluate why. Is it the photography that caught you, a fresh color combination or thought-provoking journaling? Try reading with a pad of sticky notes and a highlighter, so you can easily return to the information and inspiration that you most need.

The last two chapters go beyond the basics with a closer look at decorative accents and digital scrapbooking. In a recent interview, I was asked what makes scrapbooking so exciting. Without really thinking I said, "Scrapbooking has something for everyone." And it's true. Whether you're a beginner, yet to make your first foray into a scrapbook store, an enthusiast boasting drawers full of 3-D goodies, or a tech-savvy computer wiz with no need for scissors or paste, scrapbooking is for you. Everyone has memories; everyone has a story to tell. Scrapbooking is all about celebrating who you are moment-by-moment, page by page.

Making a Connection

In our premiere issue, I shared a story about my grandma, Addie. I had asked grandma to share her recipe for apple crisp with me, so I could scrapbook it. As I was dutifully copying down each ingredient from within a tattered recipe booklet she'd handed me, I posed a serendipitous question. "Grandma, where did you get this recipe booklet?"

"I remember that day as if it were yesterday" is how she began. The story she shared opened my eyes to the idea of scrapbooking human connections.

It was 1937. Grandma was the mother of a toddler, expecting her second child. One afternoon her friend stopped by and extended an exciting invitation: the library was hosting a demonstration of "Automatic Electric Cookery," which, coincidentally, was the title of grandma's long-held booklet of recipes.

I relived Grandma's anticipation as she described herself and her friend running hand in hand across town. I felt her excitement as she recalled seeing an amazing new invention for the first time. She could only imagine how it might change her daily life, give her more free time. I stopped her at this point and asked, "Grandma, What is 'Automatic Electric Cookery'?"

She gave me a cute, quizzical look and said, "Why, Stacy, it's my oven."

As soon as I recovered from the shocking notion that young Addie was skilled at preparing meals without an oven, I connected to her in a whole new way. I related to her situation. She was my age, busy at home with little children, and amazed at a new technology that was going to alter her very routine.

I thought of my computer, the Internet, my cell phone—conveniences that a decade ago weren't a part of my life. Today, I can hardly fathom living without them. It makes me wonder what conveniences my granddaughter will depend on. Will I cause her disbelief when I tell her I headed off to college with a typewriter?

Scrapbooking is a lot of different things to different people. At *Simple Scrapbooks* we think scrapbooking is in part discovering the ways we are connected to our past and to the people, places, and things around us. Try it. Pick up a picture, ask a few questions, and make a connection!

There's one more thing I want to give you: permission. Permission to start scrapbooking! Start wherever you want, make big fat albums or small pocket-sized books. Tell the story of your grandparents, or the day you met your best friend. Take pictures of your garden, your car, or the food at your favorite restaurant.

Make lists of your hopes and dreams, your best cleaning tips, or the things you love about your sister. Use easy, pre-made products and copy the ideas of others. Put lots of photos on a page—or just one. Do what works for you. Break the so-called rules and follow your bliss. The point here is to dive in and enjoy the process.

Life is good. Scrapbook it!

STACY JULIAN
Editor-in-Chief
Simple Scrapbooks magazine

MY EYES ARE AN OCEAN, *by Lisa King, Kelso, WA. A quiet moment celebrated forever in perfect unity —a soft palette, a sheer vellum panel, a seashell, and a photograph of a charming little girl. Focus on the aspects of your life that you really want to capture and explore.*

Gabriela Giselle
baby's
faces
February 25, 2003
3 months old

Planning a Simple Scrapbook

What exactly is a "simple scrapbook"? Does "simple" imply that it's just for beginners? Or lacking in creativity and content? Not at all! A simple scrapbook often focuses on the "non-event" aspects of your life that might get left out of other albums—relationships, hopes and dreams, daily routines, and family traditions or, it might be an album to celebrate a specific event. A simple scrapbook helps you get back to the basics and record the smaller, quieter moments in your life—the ones that really matter most in the grand scheme of things.

Capturing a week of our lives between the pages of a scrapbook can give us a "forest" perspective on the "trees" that make up our days. Through scrapbooking, we realize how much we contribute to our families and friends, to our careers and hobbies.

Every simple scrapbook follows a format of some sort. One of the key aspects of an album's format is the design scheme used throughout the album—the colors and materials, the way various elements are arranged on the pages, and so on. A consistent design scheme helps tie all the pages together and lends a strong feeling of continuity to the album.

◀ **Baby's Faces,** *by Silvia Arizaga Kolsky, Reno, NV. Using a series of mats, Silvia crops in tightly to maintain a visual interest in this adorable layout. Using different shades of pinks also provides a sense of variety while maintaining consistency.*

▶ **Esther and Edwin,** *by Shawn Ash, Vancouver, WA. This classic photo appears fresh and new with a simple floral pattern frame, border, and tags. Don't forget that the photographs should be the focus of your layouts. A single photograph creates drama naturally.*

One of the unique characteristics of a simple scrapbook is the framework—a group of pages, such as a title page and a table of contents—that provides the overall structure for the album and helps define what the album is all about. Completing the framework pages first and thereby defining the overall organization and style of the album allows the rest of the book to come together quickly with a consistent look and feel.

Cover

Dedication Page

Contents Page

Title Page

Section Page

▲ **Christmas Mini Album,** *by Amy Williams. With a color scheme of red and various hues of green, plus a few holiday embellishments, this Christmas-time album focusing on one family event is striking. Amy created a framework for her album with the title page, dedication page, and contents page to organize her pictures and journaling into a logical format.*

Remember, when creating a framework for your simple scrapbook, consistency is the number-one goal. For example, if you use letter stickers on the title page, then use them on your dedication and contents pages. The idea is to create a look and feel, establish it on page one, and repeat it throughout the book.

Creating a Framework

Title page. You'd never find an untitled book at the library (and if you did, would you check it out?). Every scrapbook needs a title page. A title tells the reader what to expect to see when looking through your album. Surprisingly, a title also gives you direction as to the scope of the album. Is it a year in the life of your family? Is it a book about a special friend or a special celebration? The title page is where you give your album a name and also list the date and other identifying information (such as your own name). This page is also the place to introduce the visual elements—papers, colors, accents—that will appear on subsequent pages. It is the title page that sets the tone and the style for your entire album.

Dedication or introduction page. A dedication or introduction page is optional, but it's a really nice, personal touch. Who is the book for? You? Your children? Your parents? A friend? A dedication page makes your scrapbook's intentions—and the intended recipient—clear. You don't have to write a lot on your dedication page, but you should definitely continue the design elements introduced on the title page.

A dedication page connects you, the maker of the scrapbook, to the readers, allowing them to see each page and each experience through your eyes.

A title page tells the reader "what" your scrapbook is about. The dedication page unlocks the mystery of "why." Why did you want to create this album? For whom did you create it? What do you hope they will come to understand through reading it? A dedication adds so much meaning to any album. The dedication does not always have to be a separate page. It is often included as part of the cover or title page.

Table of contents page. If your album is going to be divided into sections—days of the week, members of a family, holiday traditions—you might want to include a table of contents page. This optional page provides a quick overview of what's included in the album, usually listing the section titles. The table of contents might introduce a distinguishing design characteristic for each section, such as a specific color or decorative accent (die cuts, stickers, rubber stamps, etc.). This page tells people where you will take them in your album. Be sure that the elements on this page support the visual theme of the album.

Section pages. Section pages, which simply contain the section title, are used to introduce and divide each section of your scrapbook (if you're using sections). They borrow bits and pieces from your title page or table of contents, isolating elements from them in a consistent way to reinforce their purposes.

Filler Pages

The filler pages for this extended family-Christmas Eve party album by Amy Williams are filled to the brim with festive family photos. The photo mats tie the pages to the palette established in the framework pages.

FILLER PAGES. These pages fill up the album or each of the individual sections. They're the "meat" of your album. Unlike the other framework pages, filler pages don't all have to be completed at the beginning of your project. You might create only one or two initially, and add others later. The content of the pages is based on the album's organization, and the pages themselves can be as simple or detailed as you like. Filler pages also coordinate with the design of the other framework pages, although the detail is typically simpler (sometimes only a color or design element is repeated). Here you can be as creative and complex as you like.

CLOSING PAGE. Each scrapbook can be considered a chapter, an episode in the story of your subject's life. A closing page gives the reader a sense of completion and gives you a great sense of accomplishment. It gives both of you a chance to pause and think about what has just been shared. Here's where you can tell the readers exactly what you hope they have gained from viewing your album.

A closing page is optional, but it's a terrific way to add an "ending" to your book. You can include a few summarizing thoughts, a short biographical profile about yourself, an inspirational quote, or a parting photograph.

A simple scrapbook is a project you can actually finish! Chronological albums tend to be ongoing projects with an "I'll-never-be-caught-up" aspect that can add stress to our already busy lives. A simple scrapbook, on the other hand, is an album you know will be completed. Because you're working within a framework, you know exactly how many pages you need to create. Even those scrapbooks that are occasionally updated with a filler page or two can be considered complete books and can be displayed in your home—because the completed framework pages give the book a finished look and feel.

One of our favorite characteristics of a simple scrapbook is that it's fast to create. Often, the most time-consuming aspect of making a scrapbook is merely deciding what format you want to use, then creating the first few framework pages. The rest of the album—including any future filler pages—comes together quickly. All you have to do is follow the format and plug in your photos and journaling!

Organizing Your Ideas

Organizing your scrapbook supplies can be a never-ending process, but organizing your ideas doesn't have to be. You can spend less time searching for inspiration and more time scrapbooking if you use a three-ring binder to keep your ideas and notes organized and accessible.

Gather a three-ring notebook, ABC index tab dividers, and sketch paper. Prepare categories that work for you and mark them on the tab dividers (for example, A for accents, B for birthday ideas and baby).

Insert each idea or resource in the corresponding category. Use sticky notes or put a pocket in each section. Compile new ideas and resources every month and incorporate them into your notebook. Carry your notebook around with you when you attend a scrapbooking convention or cropping party. You'll have all your ideas at your fingertips.

Accordion files are also great storage tools. Stored items are protected and organized at the same time. Organize photos, ticket stubs, travel brochures—even organize paper scraps by color (including white, black, and neutrals)—so that you'll have everything you need when you're ready to start scrapbooking.

Christmas Morning, *by Karen Glenn. The textured red paper provides the perfect stage to display the photos with simple white mats and the white snowflake brads. The smooth vellum complements the texture of the red paper and the snowflakes.*

The placement of all design elements on a Simple Scheme *blueprint for a scrapbook page layout is predetermined; just plug your photos, title, journaling, and embellishments into the appropriate spots. The beauty of a scheme is its versatility. Like blueprints for a model home, you can follow the plans exactly, or modify them to fit your needs. Either way, you'll save time and feel confident with your design.*

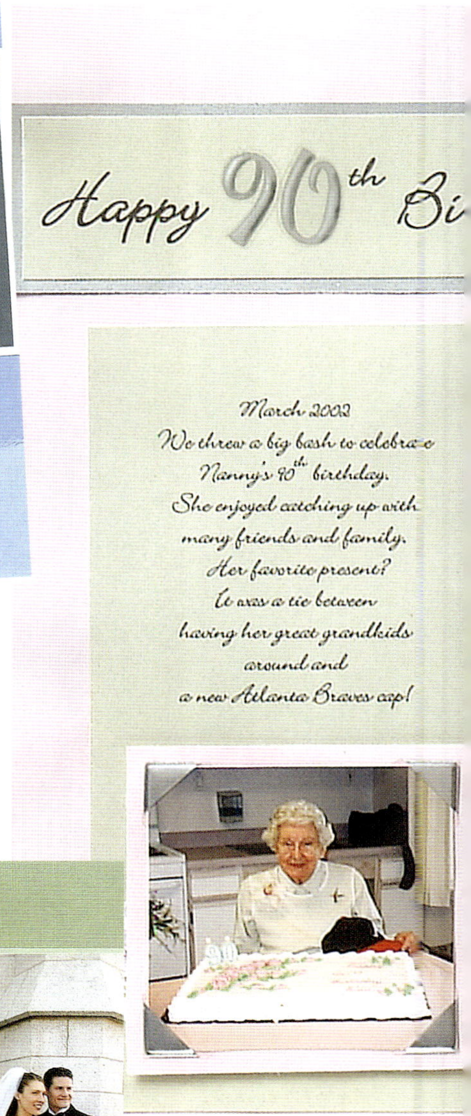

▲ **Happy 90th Birthday!,** *By Julie Parker, Cedar Hill, TN. This layout uses the same* Simple Scheme *blueprint as the one on the facing page, but Julie has opened up the flush top and bottom alignment of the photos to refocus attention on the birthday guest of honor. Using a scheme is a great way to cure scrapper's block. Limiting design choices frees you from over-analyzing every decision, while it stimulates creativity.*

◀ **Emily & Ben,** *by MaryRuth Francks, Spokane, WA. Using a* Simple Scheme *blueprint, you can easily create fast and appealing scrapbook page layouts. In MaryRuth's layout, combinations of cardstock and patterned paper replace the blue values of the background in the scheme blueprint. Remember not to let your paper choices overpower the other elements.*

A Formula for Success

We've designed a simple scrapbook "formula" to help you compile an album as quickly and easily as possible. Your answers to this short set of questions will help you determine the purpose and format of your album. Refer to the formula as you gather materials, design and create pages, and add updates to your scrapbook in the future. The formula serves as your roadmap, and will help make completing your project a snap!

PURPOSE

Why am I making this album?
Who or what am I celebrating?
What emotion do I want to capture?
How will I use this album?

FORMAT

What size and style of album will I use?
How will I organize my album?
By chronological highlights (monthly or by event)
By theme (holidays, vacations, school)
By favorite (photo I love, collections, etc.)
Alphanumerically (ABC book, top-ten list)
Question and answer (interview-style, use of questionnaire)
Other (Don't feel constrained by someone else's guidelines. Imagine the possibilities and blur the lines!)
What framework pages do I want/need to include in the album?
Title page
Dedication page
Table of contents
Section pages
Filler pages
Closing Page
Other
What is my color scheme?
Attach color swatches
What decorative accents will I use?
How will I arrange my photos and journaling on the frame work and filler pages to create a unified look and feel?
This is your design scheme.
Draw thumbnail sketches.

PREPARATION

Do I need to gather additional information?
If yes, what?
Who do I need to contact?
What photos do I need to complete the album?
Do I have all the photographs, or do I need to contact someone or take more photos?

▶ **LETTERS FROM MOM TO MY GIRLS,** *by Marjorie Scherschlig, Plymouth, MN. With a series of mats and frames, Marjorie created this special book of letters that offers variety while maintaining consistency. By adding fiber bows and eyelets, she dressed up each page while still preserving the special palette and style.*

the Scherschligt girls
lucy
table of contents
martha
eliza

AUTUMN BEAUTY, *by Carrie Owens, Sandy, UT. The playful nature of the little girl takes center-stage in this beautifully organized layout using a soft, calming color palette.*

COMING FULL CIRCLE, *by JoAnne Nielsen. Sometimes the simplest pages can be the most pleasing. Gayle's journaling, paired with the large photograph and the decorative leaf, create a balanced look. The intimate photograph brings you right into the artist's workshop.*

FISH ALL DAY, *by Jennifer Blackham, West Jordan, UT. Decorative patterned papers and stickers enhance the colors of nature. The warm natural bond of the father and sons is captured and celebrated in the perfect-summer-day photos and the decorative accents.*

Grayson, Landon
and Callahan Blackham

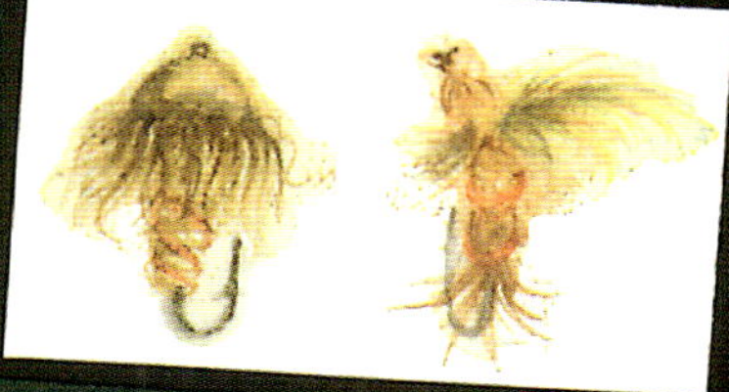

We were on a camping trip to Wasatch Mountain State Park when we discovered kids could fish free at the little pond by the golf course. We didn't catch any fish in the 30 minutes before the boys were bored, but it was fun just to be outdoors enjoying nature. I was especially glad we didn't have to fish out any boys from the water!

July 2001

Smile

Design Basics

Fortunately, you don't have to be a design expert to know how to create attractive scrapbook layouts. There are a few basic principles of design, which you can easily apply to your scrapbook pages. With a little knowledge—and your own intuition—you'll be creating well-designed pages in no time. It's that simple!

The process of design is organized into two categories: design principles and design elements. Design principles are ideals you try to achieve on a layout, such as focus, contrast, and balance. Design elements, on the other hand, are things you put on a page, and they have qualities such as color, shape, size, and line. These characteristics are found in all the things you pick up, move around, and eventually adhere to a scrapbook page—things such as photos, journaling (the words you add to the page), titles, and embellishments.

A good scrapbook designer knows how to manipulate design principles and elements to create an aesthetically appealing finished product. Incorporating both aspects of design into your layouts will help you preserve precious memories in a way that both expresses your message and captivates the viewer.

◀◀ **Smile,** *by Lisa Britchkow, Dresher, PA. This mini album cover uses three different patterned papers of contrasting colors. The hot red color draws attention to the page, and the two blues cool it down. The colors, taken from the bouquets of flowers, are a dramatic contrast to the more usual wedding pastels.*

◀ **It's Not About What You Catch,** *by Cathy Zielske, St. Paul, MN. The monochromatic color scheme helps keep the emphasis on the photos in a page that captures the nostalgia of a boy fishing with his dad.*

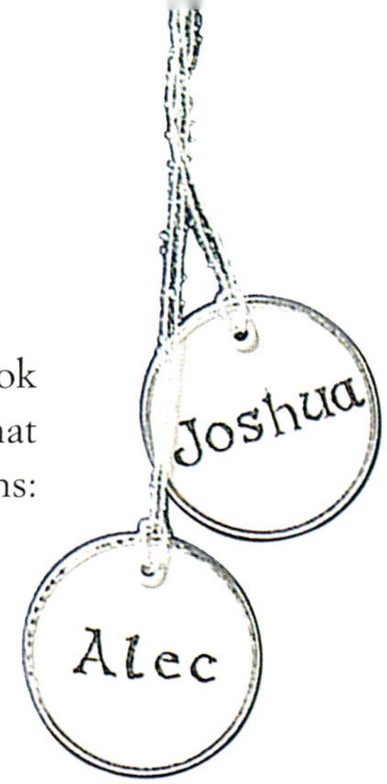

Creating a great scrapbook layout begins even before you pick up a paper trimmer or look through your cardstock supply. Your first step is to make some conscious decisions about what message you want to convey. Before you begin any project, ask yourself the following questions:

1. What is my goal for this layout? By consciously choosing a goal, you can more easily determine which photos, techniques, and embellishments will help you create a successful layout.

2. Who is the layout for? Are you writing to yourself? To the subject of the page? To future generations? Knowing your audience will help you decide what to include on the page.

3. What tone do I want the layout to have? Warm and homey? Wild and energized? Deciding on the mood will help you choose the appropriate colors and themes.

▲ **Thank You,** *by Cathy Zielske, St. Paul, MN. A "visual triangle" has been created with key visual elements in groups of three, generally with equidistant placement. The pages are further linked by the repetition of purple accent flowers and black title blocks.*

▶ **Cold Lips, Warm Hearts,** *by Karin Smith, Dundas, Ontario, Canada. Torn paper creates a wintry border for the snowman and his friends.*

Joshua
Alec
COLD LIPS WARM HEARTS
Take 2 kids, 2 inches of snow, a little imagination and a whole lot of love. add it all together and end up with a memory that Mommy will cherish for a lifetime.
Nov. 2002

◂ **FEELIN' FROSTY,** *by Alannah Jurgensmeyer, Rogers, AR. Many product lines feature complementary items that can be mixed and matched. If you're short on time, look for pre-printed enhancements that take the guesswork out of scrapbooking.*

▸ **HILARY HARKER,** *by Marnie Flores, Madison, WI. The organic swirls of the tonal yellow paper in the tag add a softness to the more rigid patterns of stripes and plaids, tying the layout together.*

The Extras

There are innumerable accents scrapbookers can use to enhance their pages. In fact, without embellishments, half of the fun of scrapbooking is lost! Whether you use the cute embellishments you find at your local scrapbook store or create your own accents from scratch, the main purpose of decorative accents is to make your page more visually interesting and to draw the viewer's eye to the focal point—or featured element—of your page.

A trip to your local craft store, fabric store—even hardware store—will reveal endless treasures just waiting to be used on your scrapbook pages. Brads, eyelets, studs, rhinestones, and many other decorative accents come in a variety of shapes and sizes. They'll help you add interest—and a classy touch—to any design.

First, however, focus on the most important elements of the layout—the photographs, of course, and your journaling. You can then step up your design by adding shapes and extra color to enhance the layout. Step it up again with even more decorative touches—punched-out letters, brightly colored patterned paper, and die-cuts, buttons, or twine.

Embellishments are important, and often essential, to your layouts. But the photos are what you want the viewer to see. Keep this constantly in mind as you're adding those extras to your pages. Remember to use care—and restraint—when highlighting photos with an accent or technique. If you don't, you run the risk of placing more emphasis on the embellishment than on the photo.

Ask yourself if your journaling block is going to shift the focus away from your featured photograph, or if the color of your embellishment is just too much against the subtle colors in the image. Embellishments are extra spices—they aren't the main ingredients of a layout. So add a little at a time and then "taste" your creation to see if it works. If you want to add more, do so, but continue to constantly reevaluate the page so that you get just the right flavor.

The Focal Point

Focal point is an important concept in design. When you decorate a room, you establish a focal point—it could be the fireplace, the bed, a window, or the television. Then you arrange everything else in the room around that focal point. The focal point anchors the room and creates a point of interest.

Designing a scrapbook page is a lot like decorating a room. You have to choose a color scheme, create a focal point, arrange furniture (the photos), and add accessories (the embellishments). Just as in a room, the focal point of a layout is the first place your eye rests. It tells the viewer where to start. It can also help her understand what you want to communicate. Each time you give the viewer a focal point, you cause her to stop. Each time she stops, she'll understand more of your message.

A focal point is the dominant image on your layout. It's most often a photograph, but it can also be a block of journaling or other important element. The focal point is set off in a way that distinguishes it from all others on the page. It commands attention first. Everything else serves a supporting role. This doesn't mean the other elements aren't important; it just means you're highlighting the element that best defines the layout. You're creating a visual signpost that says, "The story begins here."

Creating a Focal Point

9 Ideas for Take-Charge Layout Design

1. Create a Single-Photo Page. By giving a photo a page all its own, you assign it focal-point status. In any design where multiple elements are involved, visual attention is drawn to any element that is isolated from the rest.

2. Enlarge Your Focal-Point Photo. Enlarge your focal-point photo to 5 x 7" or even 8 x 10". Most reprint costs are quite affordable, or you can use the Kodak Picture Maker or Fuji Aladdin systems available at your local developer or discount retailer for a nominal fee. By enlarging the focal-point photo, you show the viewer where to look first.

3. Crop Your Supporting Photos into Smaller Sizes. Sometimes you might not have the

Winter Schminter, *by Tracy Kyle, Coquitlam, British Columbia, Canada. The large focal-point photo is closely cropped and supported by the warm yellow and orange ribbon accents.*

Marinne Turns 3, *by Amy Williams, Old Town, ME. Profile shots are often overlooked, but this focal-point photograph demonstrates how the contours of the face capture emotion and sentimentality that straight shots tend to miss.*

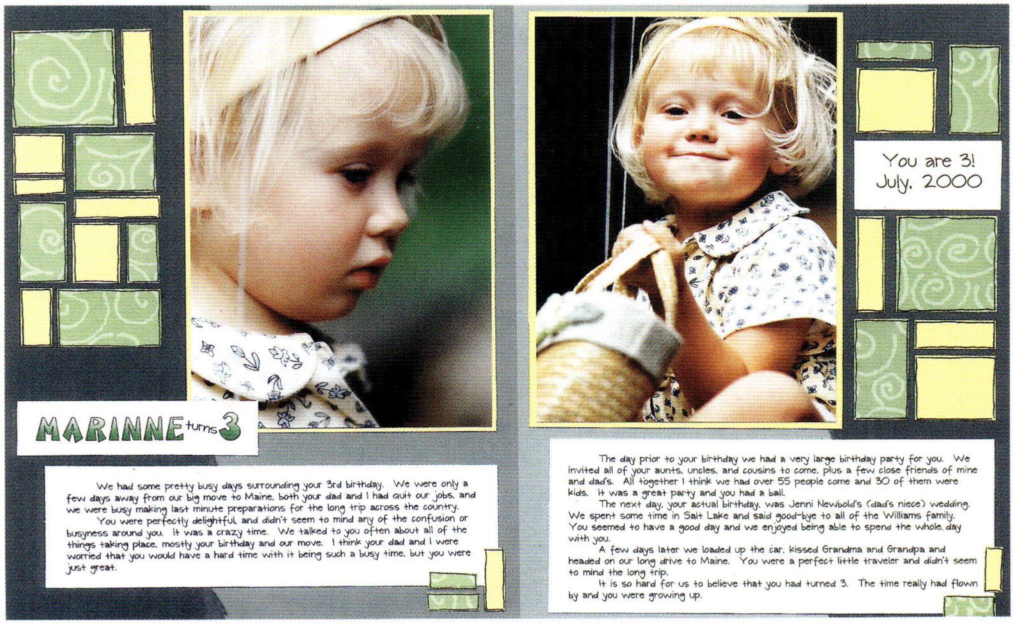

luxury of running out and making enlargements. When that's the case, crop your supporting photos so they're smaller than your focal-point photo. This is a great way to put the emphasis on one photo, while still including other shots that support the theme of your layout.

4. Mat Your Focal-Point Photo. Putting a mat behind your focal-point photo is another excellent way to draw attention to it. When the photos on a layout have a similar visual value, the one with the mat will stand out. Try double-or even triple-matting the photo for full effect.

5. Crop in Tightly. Sometimes the immediacy of a closely-cropped photo is enough to grab our attention. A tight face shot instantly engages the viewer.

6. Place It in a Prominent Position. Where you place your photo on the page can signify focal-point status. Because we read from left to right, and top to bottom, our eye naturally gravitates to the upper left portion of a scrapbook page. If the photo you choose as your focal point lacks visual interest (it's not your best photography, say), the use of placement will be even more important and very effective in emphasizing it as the starting point.

7. Place Your Focal-Point Photo Next to the Title. Use your title to draw attention to your focal point. The title can be placed above and below the focal-point photo, focusing the eye directly on the picture.

8. Use Embellishments. Place embellishments near your focal-point photo, and you give it more visual "weight." The small embellishments on the photo mat highlight the photo and complement the theme of the layout.

9. Use Pre-Made Frames. Pre-made products, especially frames, make creating a focal point a cinch. Just choose your photo, mount it on the frame, and voila—instant focal point!

◀ **MOTHER AND SON,** *by Vivian Smith, Calgary, Alberta, Canada. Notice how easily your eye spans this layout. Contrasting colors, shapes, and textures add visual appeal.*

Contrast

Contrast refers to the difference between elements that distinguishes them as unique. The resulting tension adds energy, emotion, and visual appeal to your page. In scrapbooking, you can create contrast by varying sizes, colors, shapes, textures, and patterns. You can also use this principle to emphasize your focal point.

Color and pattern are excellent ways to create contrast—and patterned papers have plenty of both. Choose a patterned paper with themes, colors, and proportions that support your photos. Add other patterns, keeping these basics in mind: Establish variety in size and design; pair big patterns with small; and combine soft, flowing, or organic lines with the regularity of stripes or plaids.

Emphasize one paper over another to create cohesion. Low-contrast or neutral patterns are good for large areas, and bold, bright, or graphic patterns work best in smaller spots.

Be sure to work with compatible styles. For example, you wouldn't match vintage florals with contemporary geometrics because the two styles don't feel the same. Also choose closely related color schemes. Because the differences in pattern create the contrast, use colors with similar values, intensities, or temperatures.

To help you get started, select a color-coordinated paper line. They're designed to work together. The colors are beautiful and the patterns alluring, but be careful not to let them upstage your photos. When mixing patterned papers, stick with similar colors to keep the focus on the photos.

Pairings

Some things are just meant to go together. Consider the peanut-butter-and-jelly sandwich: rich, creamy peanut butter on one slice of bread; sweet, fruity jelly on the other—a perfect (if not low-cal) combination. Scrapbook pages can also benefit from some strategic combinations. Rather like sandwich fixings combined on a single mat to add a delectable

touch to your layouts. Try placing your focal-point photo and title on the same mat. This arrangement adds emphasis to both key elements, allowing the viewer to take in the layout's message in one glance. Looking for some other tasty options? Try combining a photo with journaling or a page accent.

Putting elements together on a single mat can simplify the scrapbooking process and add a sense of unity to your pages. "Sandwich" some page elements on your next layout. You may find it's as enjoyable as a good, old PB and J—and a delicious addition to your album!

▼ **GRANDPA DOUG,** *by Jenny Jackson, Gilbert, AZ. The arrangement of embellishments, titles, and journaling on a page is meant to support the focal-point photos. Tighten the title by mounting it on a different shade of cardstock or patterned paper. Or try matting your journaling so that it doesn't disappear on the page.*

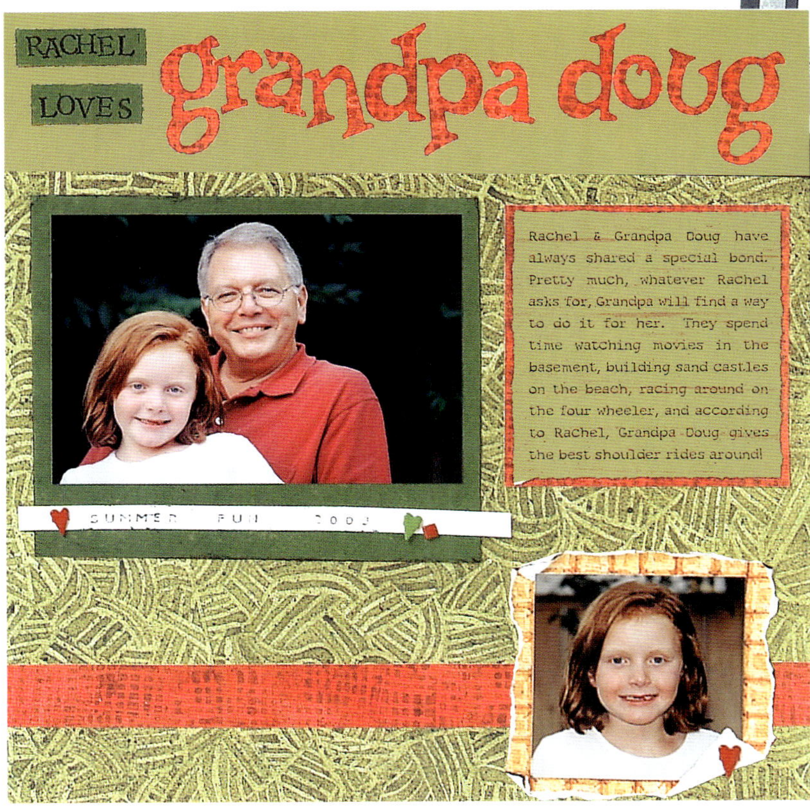

▲ **HOW IS IT POSSIBLE?,** *by Carrie O'Donnell, Newburyport, MA. The unusual point of view of the photograph—from inside the window—captures a priceless father-and-son moment.*

▸ **All Star Kids,** *by Taunya Dismond, Lee's Summit, MO. Taunya presents all the elements of a succesful layout—vibrant photos, happy-go-lucky titles, simple matting, and concise journaling. Festive decorative accents complete this celebratory layout.*

Shape

In scrapbooking, shape gives pages life and vitality. By simply adding a few geometrical shapes to a page, you create visual interest and excitement. Shape can also help you create rhythm and motion on a page. By incorporating curved lines and other loosely defined shapes into your page, you can lead your viewer's eye toward or away from a specific element. In addition, by repeating shapes on a layout, you can create a pattern that will encourage a sense of order and clarity.

Shapes can be positive or negative. A positive shape is what we generally think of when we think of shape. It's the outline of an object. A negative shape is the outline of the absence of the shape.

Sound confusing? It's really quite simple. For example, imagine laying an element down on a piece of paper and designing your page with that element in place, adding color or texture around the element to define it. Now imagine lifting that element to reveal the silhouetted shape of that element on the page.

Working with negative shapes can be an effective way to create visual interest on your page while still keeping it uncluttered. You can achieve negative shapes on your pages by using the negatives of punches—the pieces of paper or cardstock into which you've punched the shapes. You can also leave a shaped space on your background page by using templates, die-cuts, or any number of other techniques.

Try incorporating shape into your layout with a geometric mat or even with the photograph itself. For example, you can take a photograph in an environment that features strong shape, and crop the photograph tightly or silhouette the shape. Another way to integrate shape on your layout is to use embellishments that have definite shapes, such as circle tags, stickers, and punches.

If you decide to use shapes on your layout, be sure to "ground" them so they don't appear to float on the page. Imagine picking up your layout and holding it vertically. Do the shapes look like they would fall to the ground (even if fixed in place with adhesive)? If so, they need to be grounded to the page. You can ground a shape by layering items on top of it, creating a mat for it, or clustering the shapes to form a pattern.

Blowing Bubbles, *by Barbara Carroll, Tucson, AZ. Two butterfly stickers, one matted and one not, placed in opposite corners of the layout, support the charming focal-point photograph. The size, color, shape, and position of the elements on a page contribute to good balance.*

Balance

Balance is definitely something we strive for in our hectic and demanding lives. And although you may not always attain perfect balance in everyday life, you can create it on your scrapbook pages. Nothing contributes to the success of a layout more than good balance. Whether you're new to scrapbooking, a seasoned veteran, or somewhere in between, balance will help you take control of your page design. A balanced layout—one in which all of the elements are arranged so that each side of the layout weighs the same visually—creates a feeling of harmony and is more pleasing to the eye.

When it comes to balancing a layout, you have many factors to consider, including the size and shape of the elements, the visual "weight" of your photos' subjects—even the weight of colors, textures, and patterns on your page. A large object, for example, "weighs" more than a small one. A bright color weighs more than a subdued one. And an element with a pattern or texture weighs more than one without.

Symmetry

Symmetry occurs when like shapes are repeated in the same positions on each side of a vertical line. Creating symmetry is the easiest way to create balance on a scrapbook page. The simple rule is, what you have on one side of the page, you should also have on the other.

Think of it as "mirror-image scrapbooking." If you have a photo on the left, you should have a photo on the right. Two flower stickers on the right, two on the left, and so on. Another easy way to create symmetrical balance on a spread (two pages) of your scrapbook is to apply a patterned border of the same width to the outside edges of each page.

Symmetrical balance is stable, structured, and somewhat conservative (which is just fine). Consider symmetry for formal layouts, such as weddings or graduations; photo-intensive layouts (symmetry can help you get a lot of pictures down with minimal planning); and anything that requires a more restrained tone or approach.

Because it is so rooted in fixed principles and bound by propriety, symmetrical design might not seem to offer any chance for improvisation. Not true! Any design can be modified slightly and remain a symmetrical design. Symmetrical balance can be achieved even with elements that are not exactly the same, as long as they occupy the same visual space on your layout. For example, create a design on one page and simply invert the design on the facing page. The result? Modified symmetry!

Asymmetry

Asymmetrical balance requires a bit more planning than a straightforward symmetrical layout, but the results can be very engaging. With asymmetry, you create balance by arranging elements of different sizes, in different quantities, and in different positions. For example, if you position a photo on the left side of a page, you might place three smaller photos on the right side. One flower sticker on the right, three flower stickers on the left. The result: visual elements of different sizes balancing each other.

One of the keys to creating a successful asymmetrical layout is to unify the two pages of your spread through repetition. Shifting photos and embellishments off center is another way to create asymmetrical balance.

Each element in a layout has weight and size. To achieve asymmetrical balance, determine how much or how little of an element—both in number and size—will balance other elements on the page. For example, a small, dark element will "balance" a much larger, lighter element.

Determine where to place the items on the page to create balance. Don't think of your layout simply as a two-dimensional form that must balance from left to right. Rather, think of your layout as a three-dimensional object. Visualize a triangle that includes points on the left side of the layout, the right side of the layout, and your eye. The elements on your page need to balance left to right, top to bottom, and up to down.

Asymmetrical balance brings contrast, excitement, motion, and informality to a layout. It creates a more youthful, dynamic feel that works well for layouts with informal, active, or playful themes.

HOMEMADE TEDDY BEARS, *by Amy Williams, Old Town, ME. A single photo on the top half is perfectly balanced with store-bought frames and journaled tags.*

Sand, *by Donna Downey, Huntersville, NC. Use similar shapes and colors in opposite locations on your page to help establish a sense of visual balance. Here, the small gray square placed lower right offers a counterbalance to the large square upper left.*

The Rule of Thirds

If you've ever taken a basic photography class, you're familiar with the Rule of Thirds. Basically, the rule divides a rectangular space into thirds both horizontally and vertically, creating nine smaller rectangles and four points where the lines intersect. The most important elements of your composition should be placed where these lines intersect. Why does it work? Good question. For centuries, artists have relied on the rule, knowing it results in a pleasing, balanced arrangement.

This same rule applies to scrapbook pages. You can create balance and visual interest on your layout by placing the most interesting and important elements on your page at the intersection of the imaginary lines.

Divide a page into three imaginary vertical columns. Put the bulk of your visual information in two adjoining thirds, and leave the last third primarily open. You have created an asymmetrical design. Create a second design on the facing page, mirroring the asymmetrical design of the first. Now you have a created a symmetrical spread made up of asymmetrical designs.

The Visual Triangle

The eye naturally wants to connect items on a page. You can facilitate this by placing elements—photos, embellishments, or type—in a triangle that spans your page. A visual triangle repeats key visual elements in groups of three, usually with equidistant placement, to create a triangular connection.

Another option is to arrange the elements in the shape of a Z (a Z is essentially two triangles, each with one side missing). Both arrangements will naturally lead the eye throughout the important elements on a layout.

So, learn to "think triangles" to give your pages a balanced look. Rely on this basic design technique once—or multiple times—when positioning stickers, photos, or journaling boxes on the page. The imaginary triangle does not need to be exact. A general approximation will do. This tried-and-true rule is a simple way to design consistently eye-pleasing scrapbook pages.

▲ **BALLERINA,** *by Angelia Wigginton, Belmont, MS. Two photographs and an elegant title create an appealing visual triangle.*

▲ **Shell Seekers,** *by Angie Cramer, Redcliff, Alberta, Canada. The visual balance of this layout is supported by the color of the letters in the title and the top border. Notice how the colors are picked up from the photograph.*

Checking Your Balance

If your finished layout doesn't "feel" balanced to you, here's what you can do to double-check it. Step back from the layout and try to determine which element or elements are disrupting the balance. For example, is there one particular element that is too heavy compared to everything else on the page? If you still can't see why the layout feels unbalanced, try flipping the pages upside down and look again, to see if the disparate element is more obvious to you that way.

You can also mentally divide your layout into a grid pattern. Decide if each area on the grid is balanced both horizontally and vertically by another area. If not, try adjusting the placement of elements to create balance. Remember, symmetry is the easiest way to create balance in a layout.

A Balancing Act

Balance is one of those tricky things. When your layout is balanced, no one notices. When it's not, nothing else you can do will make the page work. The exercise below is one way to ensure you create a balanced layout. Try following these steps.

Step 1. *Cut black cardstock into the basic shapes and sizes you want to use on your layout. Move the shapes around on a white background until you feel the design is balanced.*

Step 2. *Choose a color scheme for your page and cut out shapes in those colors, arranging them as you did in Step 1. You may find that the colors alter the balance of the page. If so, adjust them to make the balance work.*

Step 3. *Adhere your photos and embellishments to the page, using the previous steps as a guide. You don't need to follow these steps every time you create a layout—but try it a couple of times. Soon, you'll be an expert at creating balanced layouts every time!*

foliage
foliage (fo'.le.ij) 1. leaves on a plant or tree 2. brilliant colors during Fall.
a season of change
OLD NAVY
Take ONE BOY
plus a SUNNY DAY
add FALLING LEAVES
and SEE what happens.
SMILES, LAUGHTER, and FUN!
fall
November 2002

Color

Color is magic! It can make a page pop, sizzle, soothe, or charm. It's the easiest way to express your personal style and communicate the mood and emotion of your photographs. Without a doubt, color is the most powerful element a designer can use. It can stimulate your creativity, relax your mind, and recall happy memories. Color can dictate the mood of an entire layout or establish a relationship between the elements on a layout. Many people feel that color is a complex concept, but experimenting with color is one of the best ways to boost your confidence and discover how colors relate to each other.

The Perfect Color

There's no such thing as the perfect color combination. You may not pick the same color today that you would pick next Tuesday, and that's okay. If you're spending too much time trying to discover the one "perfect" color combination, relax a little. Let yourself experiment with lots of different colors, and be careful about limiting your palette (and your creativity) with statements like "I just don't use bright colors" or "Neutral colors are boring." Your confidence with color will increase as you allow yourself to play and have fun. The good news is, color is a personal decision, and no matter what anyone tells you, you don't have to

◄ **A Season of Change,** *by Brenda Cosgrove, Orem, UT. Cool purples are punctuated by playful autumnal orange journaling blocks. Using multiple mats adds depth to the layout of triadic colors.*

► **Blowing Bubbles,** *by Martha Crowther, Salem, NH. The analogous colors used in this layout are grounded by the black and white mats and checked ribbon that tie this magical page together.*

like or dislike any combination. Listen and learn—and then be true to yourself!

Here are some basic terms that scrapbookers should know when working with color. Hue is the color itself. Value refers to the lightness or darkness of a color—the darker the color, the greater the value. A tint is a color that has been lightened with white. A shade is a color that has been darkened with black. Saturation refers to the relative brilliance or vibrancy of a color. The more saturated a color, the less black it contains.

The Color of Emotion

What is it you really want to say with your photos? Remember, each color you introduce to your design will either add to or detract from your message. There are two color properties that most strongly influence its ability to communicate an emotion or mood. One is value, how light or dark a color is, and the other is temperature, the general feeling of either warmth or coolness in a color.

Every color has a powerful emotion associated with it. There's a reason why fast-food restaurants use bright colors like red, orange, and yellow—to express speed and efficiency—and health spas use subtle, more subdued colors—to express calmness and serenity. When you choose a particular color for a layout, you're also choosing the emotion or mood that your layout expresses.

Red can convey a wide range of emotions, including anger, passion, power, and excitement. It's the most powerful color and will overshadow any other color on the page unless it's used carefully. Pink can fit a variety of moods, depending on its value. Hot pinks are energetic and youthful, while lighter pinks are delicate and sweet.

Orange is perceived as a "hot" color. It's also considered the most dramatic color—that's why it's used for road signs. Orange commands attention and also tends to convey a youthful feeling.

Yellow is the color of sunshine, light, and warmth. It's usually perceived as a happy, cheerful color. Yellow is unique because it's the only color that becomes brighter as it becomes more saturated.

Green is the color of life. It's also the color that

changes mood the most when combined with other colors. For example, blue-green is calming, but yellow-green has a lot of energy.

Blue usually is associated with water or sky. Because both water and air are essential to life, blue is seen as a soothing, stable color. In its more saturated shades, blue becomes energetic and exciting.

Purple is traditionally associated with royalty and is often perceived as rich and regal. It's also considered a color of youth and exuberance.

Brown is associated with the earth. To some people, brown may appear "dirty," but for others it evokes a natural, safe feeling.

The neutral colors include black, white, and shades of gray or beige. Most neutrals are tinted slightly with another color. Scrapbookers tend to look for the colors in their photos and repeat them on the pages. Yet the neutral "noncolors" in photographs often work best with bright colors. Neutral colors make wonderful backgrounds and provide contrast and visual "rest stops" next to more vibrant colors. The next time you're working with colorful photos and start to pull papers and accents for the page, consider a "nothing but neutrals" approach.

◂◂ **Color of Your Heart,** *by Shannon Taylor, Bristol, TN. A boisterous rainbow of colors surround the monochromatic central photograph.*

◂ **Peek,** *by Jamie Waters, South Pasadena, CA. Repetition of color and pattern are seen in the textured panel of this soft neutral page. The torn paper mat supporting the photograph teases with a hint of color.*

The Color Wheel

How you use color in your scrapbooks has a lasting effect on how your pages will be viewed now and how they will be perceived by generations to come. A color wheel can help take the gues work out of combining colors.

A color wheel helps you understand how colors relate to each other. The placement of colors on a color wheel has a scientific basis. The sequence isn't haphazard, but rather is an ordered placement that occurs naturally in a spectrum of light. When you use a color wheel to guide your selection of a color scheme, your choices will be based on proven principles of balance and harmony.

Starting at red and moving clockwise, you'll find orange and yellow, which are associated with the warmth of sun and fire. These warm colors sit opposite cool colors—blue, green, and purple—associated with water, sky, and space. Green and violet bridge the gap between the warm colors and the cool.

Working with a color wheel is not difficult. After selecting a color or two from the photographs that you decide to include on your page, find those colors on the color wheel. You can easily see if and how those colors are related to each other—and discover other colors that might also work well in the composition. Evaluate the relationship. Are they close together or far apart? How does the value and intensity of each color compare? Are they bright, muted, dark, or light?

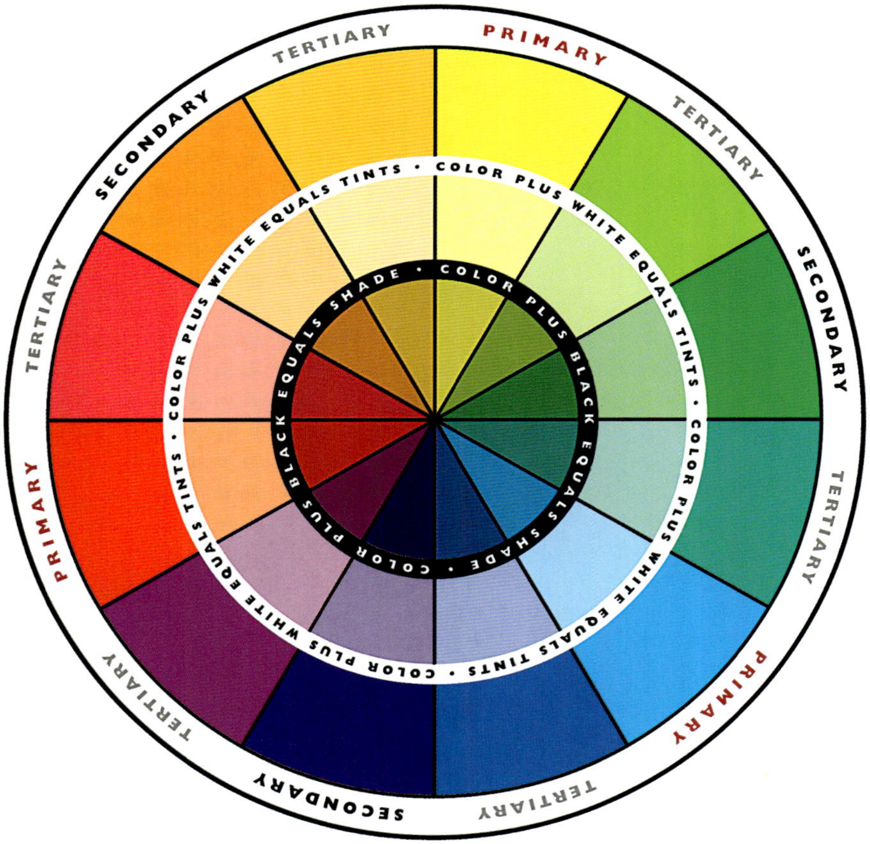

Assess whether the mood of the colors is appropriate for the message of your layout. If not, which colors would communicate the intended emotion? Consider all options by viewing the colors alongside your focal-point photo and any additional photos you plan to include on the page.

The color wheel is a handy tool that can assist you in selecting color schemes for individual pages and entire albums. Be sure to read the information on your specific wheel and become familiar with its markings and guides.

Color Schemes

Some color schemes naturally seem to work together. They likely fall into one of the categories listed here. Knowing what kind of color scheme you're using isn't absolutely necessary, but if you know what kind of scheme you're creating, you'll be more likely to create a harmonious layout.

MONOCHROMATIC. As its name suggests, a monochromatic color scheme uses only one color. You can create interest by combining an endless number of values and intensities of that color. If you're having problems getting your colors to look "just right" together, try starting with a monochromatic scheme. A simple monochromatic color scheme will keep the focus on your photos, especially if you are using many photos, or photos with lots of color. Introduce pattern and texture for added visual interest.

COMPLEMENTARY. Complementary colors are those colors directly opposite each other on the color wheel. Each pair contains a warm and a cool color, which creates a sense of natural balance. Remember that old adage that opposites attract? When you place these colors next to each other, they create a sense of vibrancy and excitement. Complementary schemes work best with strong photographs featuring few subjects. Let one complement dominate the other, or use a neutral color as a foundation and treat the complements as accents. Primary colors are a bit more intense and carry more visual weight—so keep that in mind when placing them on the page.

ANALOGOUS. Analogous colors are neighbors on the color wheel, such as green, blue-green, blue, and blue-violet. Because they are related, they create a harmonious mood and are easy to work with. Analogous colors have similar undertones and blend well together. Use a variety of lights and darks to enrich these combinations or introduce an additional adjoining color as an accent—but remember, more than three or four colors can sometimes cause your layout to lose harmony.

SOAK UP THE SUN, *by Shauna Berglund-Immel, Beaverton, OH. The analogous colors of orange and yellow convey the feeling of summertime warmth.*

◄ **ON THE ICE,** *by Karen Glen. Using the Salt Lake City Olympic logo as her inspiration, Karen used a split complementary color scheme drawing from the logo and the photographs to repeat similar shapes at the bottom for an accent.*

▼ **TIMES I TREASURE,** *by Tara Cowper, Portland, OR. Firemen wear red suspenders for a reason! Red is associated with speed and excitement. Here, the color is used in the title panel and decorative accents.*

SPLIT COMPLEMENTARY. A split complementary scheme uses a main color and the colors on either side of its complement—for example, blue and yellow-orange and red-orange.

TRIADIC. A color triad consists of three colors at an equal distance from each other on the color wheel. A triadic scheme creates a layout with high contrast because the colors are unlike each other. When used together, in the right proportions, triadic colors will create a beautifully balanced layout. However, triadic colors can sometimes overpower your photographs. For this reason, it is best to use them in varying amounts. Select one color as the foundation color; choose a second color to play a supporting role; and let the third color act as an accent. You'll have better luck combining triadic colors when they have similar values. For example, three bright colors work well together, as do three pastel colors. Put a bright color with a pastel, however, and you'll instinctively feel something is off.

Value and Saturation

Value and saturation are as important as hue when choosing colors. If you're not yet comfortable creating color schemes, be sure to stick with colors that have the same value and saturation. Value is the amount of lightness or darkness in a particular color. If you tint a color with white, you're adding lightness, thereby decreasing the value. If you shade a color with black, you're adding darkness and increasing the value. Darker colors carry more visual weight and will feel heavier on a page.

Consider this concept when using dark and light colors for pages. Does your layout feel too heavy or too light? Try mixing your values to alter their stability and vivacity.

Apply the "sink or float" principle of color. Darker colors will sink on a page, therefore they will feel more stable when used at the bottom. Lighter colors will seem to "float" and should therefore be positioned closer to the top of the page.

▲ **JEMMA'S SUNFLOWERS,** *by Tracy Robinson, Glen Waverley, Victoria, Australia. The same shapes are repeated with the added delight of the decorative sunflowers placed so they peek out from behind the photos. The black background adds a stunning dramatic note.*

Some values are easy to see—like dark green and light yellow. But if you're having trouble determining the different values of your paper, make black-and-white photocopies of them. The copies will allow you to see the gray scale, so you can easily tell which is darker and which is lighter.

The purity or saturation of a color determines its intensity. The three primary colors—red, yellow, and blue—are the purest colors of all. They are also more intense than any of the others. You cannot mix any other colors to get these three colors—but they are used to create all the other colors on the color wheel.

Different color intensities bridge different hues to each other. Mix red and yellow to get orange, red and blue to get purple, and yellow and blue to get green. These three secondary colors can now be mixed to produce the tertiary colors, such as red-purple, blue-green, or yellow-orange.

Intensity of color also affects the message of your page. Vibrant primary colors are full of life and activity and emotion. Mixed and muted colors often feel more sophisticated or serene.

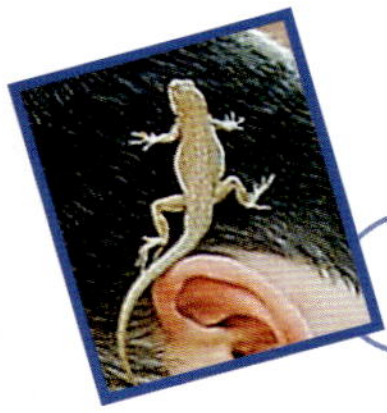

Gallon, Quart, Ounce

Using color in the right proportions on your page produces a balanced layout. You may have selected the perfect colors for your page, but the way you use those colors can make or break the layout. In general, colors are more pleasing when they're used disproportionately, or in unequal amounts. Start by choosing a single main color. Then accent the layout with one or two other colors.

◄▼ **Colors of the Sea,** *by Lisa Brown, Berkeley, CA. Compare these two pages. They are identical in layout, text, and decorative accents and differ only in the use of color. What effect does color have?*

◄ **Adventure in Arches, 2002,** *by Kim Morgan, Pleasant Grove, UT. With a monochromatic color scheme, it's easy to mix values. If you can use all colors from the same family, the page will feel like it has variety while maintaining a sense of unity.*

Essential Color Tips

1. *Work with colors you love. Be true to yourself and use your favorite colors. They will make you happy and speak to your soul. Color is something you feel.*

2. *Mix it up. Let yourself be inspired to combine colors on the cool side of the color wheel with the colors on the warm side. The result is an eye-catching contrast that adds variety to your pages.*

3. *Not all things should be equal—at least not when it comes to color. The most common color mistake is a lack of cohesion—not enough dominance of a particular mood or color to instantly tell the viewer what the message of the page is. For foolproof results every time, start with a foundation color that supports your photos and your message. Then introduce other colors carefully, a little at a time.*

4. *Repeat colors to create balance. As soon as you introduce a color with one element on your layout, ask yourself if there is an opportunity to repeat it somewhere else. Simple repetition will direct the eye and give your designs a sense of visual flow.*

... a perfect golden afternoon ...

Our home in Lewiston was surrounded by miles of farmland.
Each year we had corn, winter wheat, and alfalfa
growing near our house. One day we took a walk
down the field road through the grain.
Melissa, age four, August 1999.

If you try to use the same amount of three different colors on your page, you run the risk that the viewer will only see the color, not the page and its meaning. Here is a simple guide for using color in the right proportions. It's called the "gallon, quart, ounce" approach.

Gallon: Start with a main color. It may be a color that you have chosen from your photo or a color that corresponds with the mood, style, or message that you want to convey in your layout. Consider this as your base color.

Quart: Choose one or two additional colors that work with your base color. When selecting these colors, consider value and saturation, too. These supporting colors can be used for matting photos, creating titles and journaling blocks, and in embellishments. Don't forget to look for supporting colors in pre-designed paper and pre-made accents, too.

Ounce: Consider adding colorful brads, buttons, or other embellishments to enhance the color scheme of your layout. These items are perfect for adding that little splash of color to balance a page.

Think Inside the Box

How many times have you been encouraged to "think outside the box"? Breaking out of traditional ways of thinking is supposed to help us spark our imaginations and come up with new solutions to old problems. But sometimes thinking "inside the box" can be just as great a spur to creativity—at least, when it comes to color blocking.

Scrapbookers use a technique called color blocking to create strong rectangular shapes of color to provide lively, attractive backgrounds for photos, journaling, and embellishments. It's a quick way to add impact to your pages—and you may just find it's a technique you can't live without!

Color-blocked pages are simple to create and often don't need any additional accents—just your favorite photos. Try varying the size and number of the blocked areas, and experiment with different color combinations. As always, be sure the colors you choose support rather than detract from your photographs.

Arrange photos, journaling, and embellishments within the colorful boxes. Or allow accents to overlap the box edges to enliven the linear composition. Smaller boxes are also a great way to showcase small stickers and other elements that might get lost in a larger area.

Create an entire background with blocks of cardstock in different colors, shapes, and sizes. To add visual interest, consider crinkling one color of cardstock before adding it to your color-block layout. When using color-blocked designs, always be sure that the borders are even. Even a small difference will cause your layout to look unbalanced.

◄ **A Perfect Golden Afternoon,** *by Kiyoko Walkenhorst, Bluffdale, UT. If you decide to center a single image on the page, make sure to pay attention to the line length and the arrangement of your journaling. This centered descending line length keeps the focal point on the beautiful photograph in this exquisite layout.*

brothers
buddies
brothers
Zack & Jake
July 4 · 2002

JOY, *by Stacy Julian, Liberty Lake, WA. The unexpected light green adds a surprise element to this homey page. With red and white gingham trim and holly, this Christmastime page is filled with holiday cheer.*

ZACK AND JACK, *by Karen Glen, Orem, UT. Strong color blocks offer great support to a single photograph. The decorative accents of torn borders, colorful brads, and natural fibers all pull the layout together.*

SNOW, *by Amy Stultz, Mooresville, IN. Color not only grabs the eye, but it aids in determining the theme and emotion of your scrapbook page. The dominant icy blues in Amy's layout—evidenced in the photos, paper, and floss accents—lend to the illusion of frozen-in-time winter moments, the relative stillness of that season.*

The Joy of Discovery
wind through the leaves
birds singing in the trees

◀ **THE JOY OF DISCOVERY,** *by Angelia Wigginton, Belmont, MS. The simple dark brown cardstock with a lightly textured background along with the double mats of pale paper and vellum create interesting dimension to this outdoor layout.*

▶ **GARDENS,** *by Stacy Julian, Liberty Lake, WA. Place can take precedent over people. Scrapbook a favorite spot, bringing alive the magical colors.*

▼ **WHAT A SILLY FACE!,** *By Shauna Deveraux, Athens, GA. The cheerful green and white accent paper makes us smile just as much as Corey's silly faces. Using a patterned paper next to large photos helps to balance the layout.*

▶ **REMEMBER THIS,** *by Briana Fisher, Milford, MI. The vintage look of this page is carried through from the soft palate of the photograph to the torn paper and tinted tags.*

▶ **MYRTLE BEACH, 2002,** *by Donna Downey, Huntersville, NC. The bold color of the page presents the wonderful, closely cropped baby photo.*

▼ **MEMORY,** *by Emily Tucker, Matthews, NC. To increase visual interest, consider using different values of a color as well as varying the contrast in line (both torn and cut edges).*

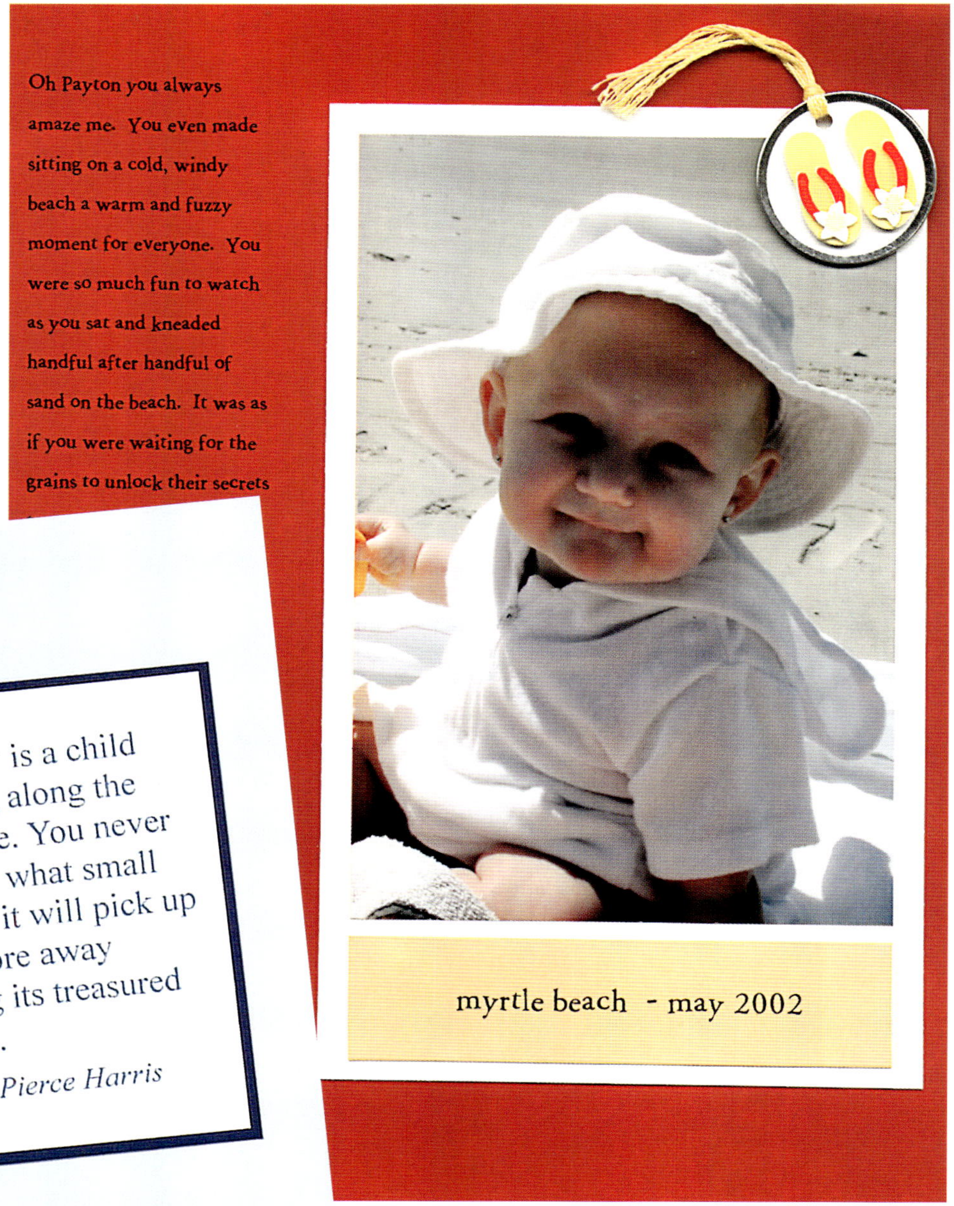

▶ **I'LL GO IN IF YOU DO,** *by Theresa Banks, Seal Beach, CA. Bright-blue patterned papers provide a visual counter-balance to the sparkling water in the photo. The blue sets the stage for the dominant image of the black puppy and his young pal.*

Boy
Sunny
Pool
Summer
Dog
Hot
Grass
Toys
Backyard
"Well Amaya, I'll go in if you do!"
Maxfield and Amaya trying to
decide who goes in first.
July 2000

Be...

original
charismatic
true

spirited
charming
sensitive
outgoing
understanding
joyful
spontaneous
determined

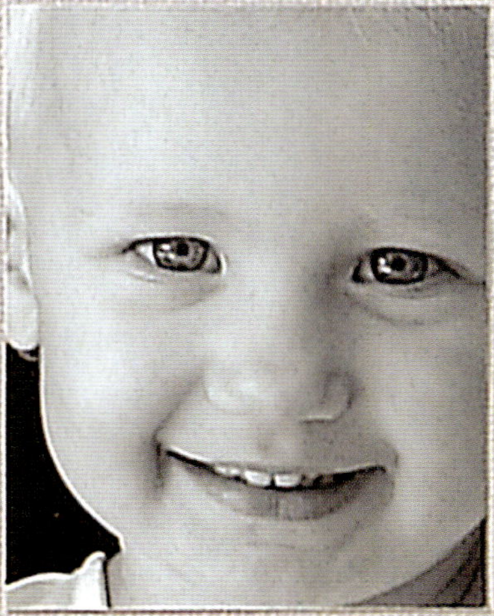

Photos

Photographs really do make a difference. The quality certainly matters—clear, crisp, well-lit photographs are the goal of every scrapbooker—but variety also matters. In any design process, whether it's creating a floral bouquet or decorating a living room, variety and contrast are essential to an interesting, successful outcome. Scrapbooking is no different. Including an assortment of photographs is one of the most important things a scrapbooker can do to present a visually descriptive and complete story in a scrapbook.

Getting a Great Shot

A close-up shot focuses on a facial expression or mood. Get up close and personal with a zoom lens. Select objects that can work to frame the subject of your photo—and include a detail or a part of the setting that helps tell the story. Show some action. A child interacting with a pet, for example, is a terrific way to highlight other family members. Capture life's spontaneity when taking playtime photos. Be sure the subject is focused on the activity, and not on the camera.

One time-honored approach to composing shots that remain in the mind's eye is to frame the subject you're shooting. Tree branches, doorways, arches, and windows, when placed in the foreground, direct viewers toward the subject. These types of framing devices lend a feeling of depth to the photograph. Frames can also conceal an uninteresting sky or any other less interesting or appealing elements of the background or the subject.

You can make a great portrait any time, any place, just by paying a bit more attention to detail.

▲ **A Cowboy Kiss,** *by Maureen Spell, Carlsbad, NM. Frame your photos and draw attention to important parts of your page by using a bright color against your white background.*

◄◄ **Be Yourself,** *by Donna Downey, Huntersville, NC. Using a neutral background like this soft mauve creates a delicate canvas on which to place the charming momochromatic photos.*

NATE

You can create more interesting photos for your scrapbook page simply by shooting from different and unexpected angles and vantage points. Don't let yourself get caught in one mode of photo taking. If your photos are always close-ups, you won't ever be able to document your surroundings. Similarly when all you have are action shots, your scrapbook may lack emotion.

When taking photos, vary the distance between you and your subject. Zoom in, zoom out, and use both horizontal and vertical orientations. Shoot pictures of people when they're not posing.

Close-up photos are great, and create a marvelous page. But a well-balanced scrapbook offers a variety of layouts, some with close-up photos and some with longer views.

▲ **NATE,** *by Tara Whitney, Valencia, CA. This horizontal layout is a great method to display a series of photos. Placing accent colors behind the photographs allows for just enough color to break through to unify the layout.*

▲ **GLIMPSES OF CHRISTMAS,**
by Joycelyne Hayes, Trabuco Canyon, CA. This parade of small squares highlights the details of a Christmastime celebration. Smaller photos are a great way to weed out the un-interesting backgrounds in many photographs.

Group Shots

When taking group shots, have your subjects interact in interesting ways. Include arresting backdrops, unique clothing and props, or a beloved family pet. Or shoot from different angles, rejecting the straight-on, eye-level perspective.

Be willing to experiment. Find ways to promote the feeling that the group is in its natural element. Seek friendly environments and familiar trappings, which will create a sense of unforced intimacy. The photo should be a natural extension of the solidarity of the group—and a signature statement for each of the individuals in it.

Nothing
Sweeter

The Five W's

Grade-school children—and journalists—learn all about the 5 W's when they are learning to write an effective narrative. Who, what, when, where, and why. Have you ever thought to consider the 5 W's while you're taking pictures at an event?

WHO? Who is this event for? Who were the participants? And who organized it?

WHAT? What is the event or occasion? What did people do there? How did you prepare? Consider the possibility that photos without people in them might best capture the "what."

WHEN? When did this event occur? Can you visually date the gathering by looking at your photographs? Are there seasonal reminders, like holiday decorations in your home or falling leaves outside the window? If the time of day is meaningful, as it would be with the birth of a child, for example, could you somehow incorporate a clock into the picture?

WHERE? Where was this event held? Is location an important component? If so, use your camera to visually capture your surroundings. Can you step back and fill your frame with the room you're in or with the surrounding landscape?

WHY? Why is this event important? Pictures that answer the "why" question largely concern emotions, feelings, and personal reactions. The look of surprise on Christmas morning, the wonder as a child discovers the world around her, that expression of anxious confidence on the first day of school—photos that capture these feelings are the photos that add special meaning to your events.

◀ **NOTHING SWEETER,** *by Cheryl Bahneman, Acworth, GA. Pictures taken in the early morning or evening when the sunlight is soft create an effect that's enchanting, enhancing the whimisical nature of a child.*

Cropping Photos

By trimming away, or cropping, unwanted parts of a photograph, you can focus the viewer's eye on the subject. Eliminate distracting background elements to create an interesting shape that is pleasing to the eye. But don't overdo it. Take care not to cut out people or things you may later regret.

One of the most basic ways to crop photos is with a template. Templates are available in a variety of shapes and sizes and are easy to use. Position the template over the photo so the subject is centered in the middle of the template. Trace around the inside perimeter of the template with a photo-safe pencil. With a pair of sharp scissors, cut out the shape and mount the photo on your scrapbook page. (Before cutting your photographs, be sure you have another copy—or at least have the negative. And be sure not to cut your only copy of a heritage or heirloom photograph that can't be replaced.)

To create an effective photo collage, crop your photos into a variety of simple geometric shapes. Or, consider cropping several photos to the same size and laying them out "filmstrip style" along the bottom of your layout.

Feature Your Photos

Photographs are the heart of your scrapbook, and there are many ways to size, position, and arrange them to tell your story.

Begin simply. Let your favorite photo take center stage. Enlarge it for an even more dramatic look. Or place the photograph next to the title. A title placed above and below a photo, for example, focuses the eye directly on the picture. Stickers, stamped images, and other embellishments arranged near your featured photo will give it more visual weight. They also complement the theme of the layout.

Frames make it a cinch to feature your favorite photo. Just choose your photo, place the frame over it, and you've created an instant focal point for your page. You'll find a number of wonderful frame designs online and at your local scrapbook supply store.

▲ **SHE LOVES ME,** *by Jill Beamer, Vancouver, British Columbia, Canada. One color, even in different shades and tints, can sometimes be too much for your layout. Jill added touches of white to create places for the eye to rest in this monochromatic page. The white pulls all the elements together—title, journaling, and most important, the photo.*

▶ **GLEE,** *by Renee Camacho, Nashville, TN. The photo is strong enough to retain focal-point status against vibrant or quiet colors.*

gleE
glee

Matting Photos

Matting photos—placing them on solid-colored or patterned paper or cardstock—is one of the most basic techniques scrapbookers use to create eye-catching layouts. Whether clean and simple or highly decorative, mats not only look great, but they also serve an important purpose on the page. You can mat simply to frame your photos and set them off from the background, or you can mat your focal-point photo to give it special emphasis. When there are several photos on a page, the one with the mat will always stand out.

Mats can also reinforce the color, mood, or theme of your page. Choose colors that enhance your photos and reinforce the mood of your layout. Take care that your mat is not so large, bright, or busy that it becomes distracting. Most often a simple mat is best. If you have trouble choosing, try laying your photo on different backgrounds and see what strikes you. Don't stress about it—there's never only one good color choice!

To mat a photo, select the width of your mat (1/8 to 1/4 inch usually works well). With a permanent, photo-safe adhesive, adhere your photo to the corner of a piece of cardstock or patterned paper, leaving the desired amount of paper showing on two sides (eyeballing the measurements works just fine). With a paper trimmer—or a craft knife, cutting mat, and ruler—trim the remaining two sides.

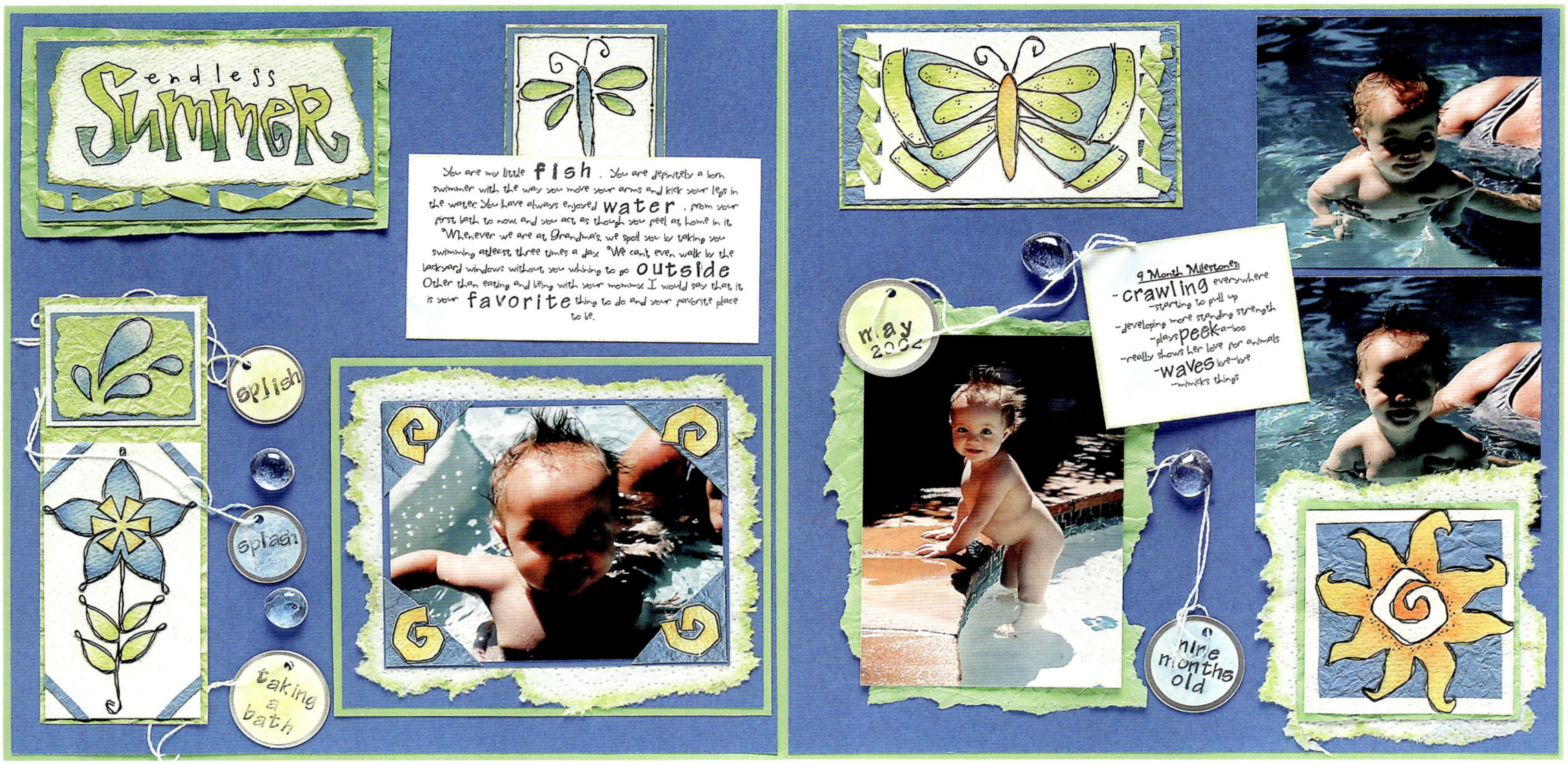

▲ **SISTERS,** *by Brook Gibbons, Bountiful, UT. Color mats tie this layout together. The focal-point photo is layered with two large, elegant torn-paper color mats—one violet and one pink—while one color from the focal-point photo is used for a small mat with each of the secondary photos.*

◄ **ENDLESS SUMMER,** *by Laurel Gervitz, Lubbock, TX. While mats present the photo, frames enclose it. This delightfully busy layout uses equally delightfully busy mats, frames, and other embellishments to capture the essence of a summer day at the pool.*

Matting possibilities are endless, so let yourself get creative. Extend one side of your mat to allow room for a title, journaling, or creative accent. Cut several mats and arrange a color-blocked design for a bold effect. Create a feeling of movement with a mat made of punched squares in a variety of colors. Fashion a photo pocket by folding up the bottom of a vellum mat.

One of the most annoying imperfections in our photos is a distracting background element that you did not notice because you were looking at the subject and not the whole frame! You can't retake the picture after you've seen the mistake, but you can cover the flaws with a creative torn-paper mat. Simply decide how much of the photo you want to hide, grab a sheet of cardstock, and do some precision tearing. Torn paper works well because it's casual and random, which adds a unique charm to the overall layout.

One of our favorite quick and easy techinques is strip-matting. To strip-mat your photos, simply crop them to the same size and mount them side by side (or vertically) on one piece of paper. Trim around them as if they were one photo and adhere them to your layout. The simplicity of strip-matting is a striking and sophisticated way to display pictures on your pages.

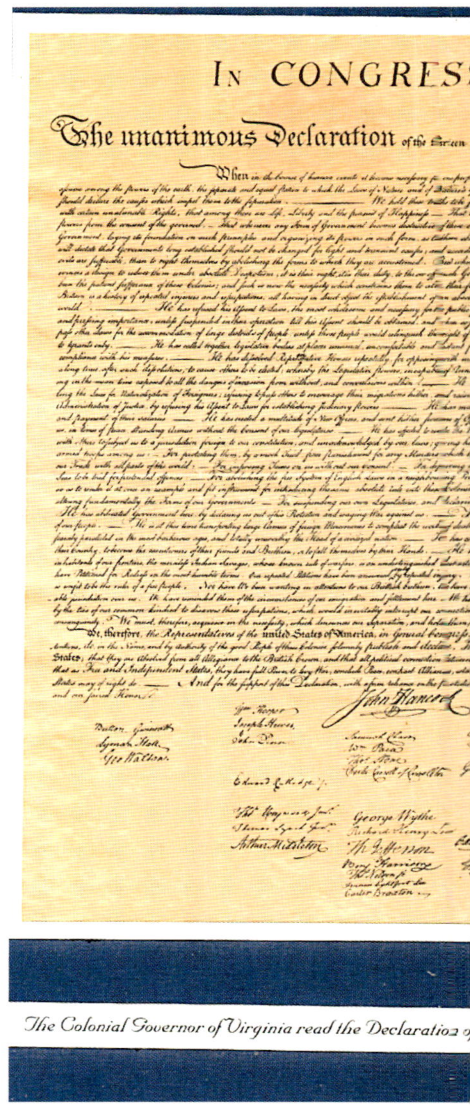

▲ **EXPRESSIVE,** *by Karen Glenn. For those times when the mood is quiet and contemplative, use subtle color combinations that connote the earthy tones of sandy beaches, country fields, or deep mountain trails.*

▶ **TRIMMING THE TREE,** *by Donna Downey, Huntersville, NC. Nothing captures the spirit of the Christmas season like the nighttime illumination of a Christmas tree. Experiment with your camera at this time of year to place your display in its best light.*

▼ **A COLONIAL INDEPENDENCE,** *by Louise Erekson, Chantilly, VA. The horizontal stripes of this patterned paper are similar to a colonial American flag. Printing famous documents, quotes and logos from the internet is an easy way to incorporate interesting clippings into your pages.*

▲ **SPARKLE,** *by Tammy Krummel, Hancock, IA. Nothing captures the spirit of winter more than close-up photos of a child enjoying the snow. The warm red palette adds to the excitement.*

▶ **ONLY TIME WILL TELL,** *by Jill Beamer, Vancouver, BC, Canada. Three different types of patterned paper in neutral colors provide a natural mat for this gorgeous photograph. The black-and-white ribbon accent supports the black and white photo.*

▸ **SOMETIMES IT'S THE SMALLISH THINGS,** *by Amy Stultz. Ordinary cardstock with a torn edge disguises the flaws of an otherwise charming photo. Torn paper works well because it's casual and random—adding to the casual feeling of the overall layout. Remember that you don't have to exclude a photograph just because it has a distracting background.*

◂ **BRUSH YOUR TEETH,** *by Jess Atkinson, Harrisburg, PA. Mats add shape to a layout and mask unwanted areas of a photo.*

SNOW DAYS

FUN
Snow Angels
Hot Cocoa
SMILES
JUMPING ON SNOW COVERED TRAMPOLINE
SnowMen
ice cycles
COLD
SNOW BALL FIGHTS
Runny Noses
Snow Ball Fights
SNOWY DELIGHT - snow vanilla sugar milk
Toasty Fires

MEGAN'S SNOW DAY MEMORIES - JULY 2002
PHOTO OF MEGAN TAKEN DECEMBER 2000

Journaling

Authentic journaling is a great way to make your scrapbooks more meaningful. Incorporate a journal into your daily routine and then add your entries to your scrapbook page. Jot down special moments or random thoughts you're likely to forget by the time you finally sit down at the end of the busy day. Sometimes the smallest details can convey the most powerful emotions.

Keep it simple—a sentence or two or even just a few words that might trigger your memory later. Jot down your first impressions of a person or place as quickly as you can. Your personal responses to everyday events say a lot about who you are. What do you like best about someone? Has anyone said or done something special for you? If so, write about it.

Record what you hear, see, smell, where you are, what you are doing, and who is with you. When you make your scrapbook page, add some of your notes next to a photograph or feature the journaling on a page of its own.

Think of three words that describe your life today. Find a photo that illustrates each of these words and put them side by side on a scrapbook page.

Find a baby photo of yourself. List five feelings you have when you look at it. Put the photo and your thoughts on the scrapbook page.

Consider creating lists of the things you love, random family memories, or things you would like to do someday. Each item on a list of things you love tells something about you and gives others the opportunity to connect with an aspect of your personality. Highlighting one of your hobbies on a layout is an ideal way to share your passion and express why you enjoy it.

◄ **Snow Days,** *by Annette Mortensen, Greensboro, NC. A clever collage of splashy colors, rough textures, oddly snipped cardstock and off-the-cuff journaling all contribute to a marvelously effective page.*

►▲ **Ten Things,** *by Angelia Wigginton, Belmont, MS. Everyone can respond to this bit of childhood magic. The quiet style and palette is reminiscent of a simpler world.*

Incorporating your journal entries into your scrapbook will bring a fresh approach to your scrapbook projects. The journaling on your scrapbook pages will be a meaningful record of who you are, and the time you live in—and that's something worth keeping.

Write from the Heart

When it comes to writing about people we love, even expert writers get stuck. Why? There's just too much to say. People are complex, as are our relationships with them. Trying to incorporate all our memories, feelings, and intimate knowledge of a person into just a few paragraphs or a few words can be overwhelming.

The truth is, not many people—except maybe immediate family members—get that much space in your scrapbooks. So when you make pages about those people who really matter to you, it's important to do right by them in your journaling.

Why not say it in a letter? Letters create intimacy, because they are directed to specific people, not an unknown audience. You can also get away with saying things you might not say in person. Use a letter to praise (or gush about) your loved one's good qualities, say what he or she means to you, and reminisce about some of your favorite, shared memories.

Another fun way to write about people you love is to pretend that you're an advertising copywriter hired to write an ad about them. It's easy to get ideas. They're all around you—in magazines and newspapers, on billboards, trucks, and T-shirts. Decide what type of ad would work best for your subject, and then be creative with the journaling. Try writing a personal ad, celebrity profile, or TV commercial for someone you love.

Or write about people you love by comparing them to something else. What person, place, or thing do they remind you of?

The Man Behind the Daddy, *by Candy Gershon, Fishers, IN. The bright red heart seals with a kiss a tender page telling a daughter about her dad before he was a father.*

Sometimes including a poem or quote can help you convey thoughts and emotions that are difficult to express. If you're searching for inspiration, for just the right turn of phrase, or for that one special saying, they're just a click away. Many books and Web sites offer a wide range of quotable quotes, sayings, and phrases that will add the perfect finishing touch to any scrapbook page.

▲ **Infinite Possibility,** *by Amy Sorensen. A photograph of an object and other favorite pictures can create unexpected connections.*

▶ **Dip, Hop, Jump,** *by Stacey Stattler, Toledo, OH. Instead of using traditional mats for these photos, Stacey creates visual interest by adding sliced borders around them.*

Adding Other Voices

You can also invite other "voices" into your scrapbooking by gathering the journaling of family members and friends. Invite them to speak to you about a past event or write something about the subject of your page—high school days or a favorite holiday, random memories of vacations, fun times at home. You may receive responses in a variety of forms, including handwritten notes, e-mails, or even verbal replies. Sorting through the responses will help you determine how to handle them.

For a uniform look in your scrapbook, you may decide to enter all the responses into your computer. Choose a font that has a handwritten look before printing out the journaling. Cut the quotes apart or use them as a single block. Be sure to save each handwritten sample, too—tuck them behind the scrapbook pages in their page protectors.

If you want to make your journaling more meaningful, start thinking like a reporter. Listen for and record the sound bites! When you take notes of words and phrases spoken by the subjects of your pages, you'll find you have a treasure trove of journaling jump-starts to work with. And, when you record the dialogue of your subjects, you reveal a tremendous amount about who they are. From the mundane to the disarming, these insightful bits of commentary often accurately tell more about your subject than page after page of text could ever convey.

Keep a notebook handy to record the silly, quirky, tender, and endearing things the people in your life say. When a child says something wise—or funny—put it into your notebook for use at a later date. By keeping the journaling in the subject's own words, you skirt the problem of wondering what to say. The people in our lives provide a wealth of journaling materials—if only we are aware enough to listen.

When you have the journalists' skill of "getting the good quote," you have two choices as to how to incorporate the spoken words into your journaling. One approach is to start with a quote or memorable wordplay and then find the photographs to support the journaling. This approach should not be stressful! The photos do not have to be taken at the time the words were actually spoken. Or you can select your photos first and then choose some appropriate quotes.

TIP: Building a collection of personal quotes is a great resource for scrapbook journaling. Recording a brief portion of actual dialogue sometimes eliminates the need to write extensively to capture the memory.

▲ **RYANSPEAK,** *by Amberly Beck, Meridian, ID. Children embellish language with such energy. Here's a great way to capture those endearing vocabulary words. Amberly highlighted her son's unique pronunciations on colorful vellum.*

◀ **BLADES OF GRASS,** *by Lisa Dickinson, Farmington, NM. Emphasize key words in a quote by printing them on contrasting cardstock in a different font*

Finding the Time

You may think that journaling requires prolonged planning and time-consuming execution, right? Not at all. Like any project, it requires just three steps.

1. Stop. When you happen upon a photo or other memory trigger and are greeted with a rush of emotion, pause to consider its significance.

2. Drop. Put down or push aside whatever else you are doing. Trust us, you can eek out a few minutes from even the busiest days.

3. Write. With a pen or a computer, record how you feel. Don't worry about how it sounds or how wayward the grammar. Just put your thoughts on paper.

Don't feel pressured to complete your journaling and design your layout in one sitting. They're two separate processes that each require your full attention. If you have to write your journaling one day and create the page design the next, that's fine.

▲ **Favorite Things,** *by Tiffany Roberts, Bonney Lake, WA. A tumble of words strewn on the page has a pleasing order all its own.*

▲ **DEAR SANTA,** *by Tracy Kyle, Coquitlam, BC, Canada. The note to Santa (top left) written in Tristan's own hand is preserved forever.*

In Your Own Hand

Aren't computers handy? From e-mail to online banking, they make so many aspects of our lives simpler. When scrapbook journaling, however, is it really easier to trek over to the computer, size a text box, and sort through a hundred fonts for the perfect look?

Instead, why not reach for a pen and simply record your memories by hand? Journaling by hand can at first seem intimidating, and it won't look as flawless as that "perfect" font. But it is guaranteed to add a personal touch like nothing else can. Be sure to include it on at least some of your pages.

You can do it. Grab that pen. Invest a little more of yourself in the journaling that informs your pages. If you're worried about mistakes, write on a separate sheet of paper or cardstock and then adhere it to your layout. Your story will gain added prominence, and if you make a mistake, you can simply cut a new oval or rectangle and journal again, rather than take your entire layout apart.

Experiment with different styles of pens. Using a variety of tips changes the look of your writing and adds visual interest. Sloppy or neat, your writing style is as unique to you as a fingerprint—something your ancestors will recognize and cherish. It carries to the reader a bit of your personality. Embrace its quirkiness. Then, take a deep breath, cast off your "my handwriting is awful" phobia, and begin to use your own handwriting in your scrapbooks.

In the Morning, *by Tara Whitney, Valencia, CA. A loving handwriten note from mother to child cradles all the gentle "babyness" in its journaled message, soft palette, and balanced layout.*

I Love Your Smile, *by Angelina Schwarz, New Castle, PA. The handwritten message on vellum with highlighted words reinforces the title of the page—I love your smile!*

As you plan the placement of photographs and embellishments, consider where you want your journaling to be positioned. Treat your journaling as a design element rather than an afterthought. Here are a few ideas to incorporate good design into your handwritten journaling.

Make your journaling part of a visual triangle. The imaginary lines between three similar elements allow the eye to flow easily across the page. Do you have a layout that uses two oval-shaped pictures? Journal in an oval-shaped space and place it accordingly. You might write your story on a piece of colored cardstock that matches two other photographs' mats, and then arrange all three in a triangle. Or, your journaling itself can form the three points of a visual triangle. Break the story into three paragraphs and place them in a triangle that spans the page. This technique can also lend a sense of chronology to a layout that covers a long time span.

Connect your layout's design theme to your journaling with embellishments. A sticker or die cut placed next to a journaling block will draw the eye to your writing. Are you scrapbooking photographs of kids flying kites? Make your journaling space kite-shaped, and you've connected the layout's theme to its content. Or, try repeating a design element found elsewhere on your page. For example, use the same type of letter in your title and as the first letter in your journaling. Visual repetition pleases the eye and invites the reader into your journaling block.

Do something fun with the words. No one said writing had to be straight all the time, so give your journaling some swoop! Add curvy lines to a boxy layout by drawing wavy lines in pencil and using them as a guideline for your words. Another fun technique? Write part of your story with a different pen color, or change pen colors to emphasize key words.

Rules of Alignment

You've just created your journaling block, and now the moment of truth: Do I center it? Justify it? Align it to the left? The alignment you choose will affect how someone reads your words. Align to the left when you have a large journaling block. A left-aligned text block (also called "ragged right") is the

The Way To Know Life, *by Lori Allred, Bountiful, UT. This sticker quotation laid over a snowy-day photo makes a bold graphic statement.*

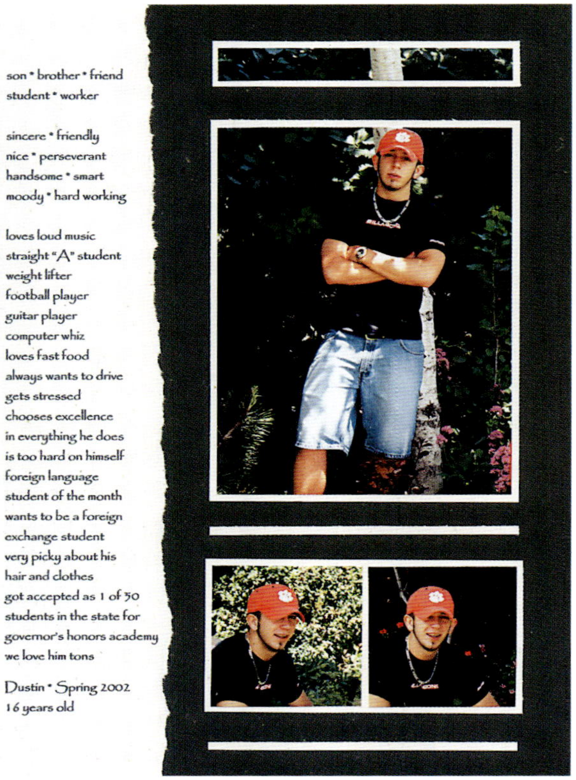

SON, BROTHER, FRIEND, *by Yvonne Schultz, South Jordan, UT. The panel containing the focal-point photo and two smaller photos is balanced by a narrower column of journaling.*

easiest of all alignment styles to read, especially when you have lots of text. For this reason, most magazines format their text using a left alignment. When in doubt, align to the left.

Centering your text is okay if the text is brief. Centering is great when you are using a quote or other journaling with eight lines or less. Pay attention to your line lengths. Centered text blocks look more appealing when the line lengths vary, fully emphasizing the centered alignment.

Justifying text, or forcing each line to be the same length, is tricky. Inevitably some lines will have fewer words, which will cause them to appear more open and spaced out than others, leaving larger gaps between words. This irregular spacing creates an uneven, discordant look. If you have similar-sized words, or you're comfortable shifting words from line to line to adjust the number of words per line, give it a try.

Decorative Lettering

Handwriting and computer printing are not your only choices for creating journaling blocks and page titles. Letter templates are another, easy-to-use option for creating decorative letters and words that are perfect for your layout. They are available in countless styles, and the letters are fun to customize. Just add beads, ribbon, or whatever else suits the style of the page to liven them up.

Add more color and emphasis to your titles by mounting template-cut letters on a torn strip of a contrasting-colored paper or cardstock. To make lettering that sparkles, trace template letters lightly in pencil directly on your page. Cover the pencil lines with double-stick tape. Sprinkle on flocking, glitter, or bitty beads, and shake off the excess.

You can also use letter templates as you would stencils. Stipple watercolor paint onto the letters with a damp brush, working from the outside of the letter inward so the paint doesn't bleed under the template edges.

For a three-dimensional effect, dry-emboss the letters. Place a piece of vellum on top of the template and gently press around the edge of each letter with a stylus. Lay brightly colored or patterned paper under the vellum to bring out the letter shapes.

Titles That Stick

Letter stickers are another great way to brighten up your journaling and your page titles. They eliminate the need to handwrite, type, cut, or glue—and allow you instead to focus on your creativity. Letter stickers are quick and easy to use and make charming titles just as they are. But if you want a little extra pizzazz, add shades of color, stamped designs, original artwork, punched shapes—or even more stickers. (Be sure to do all your embellishing while the letter stickers are still on the backing sheet. That

▲ **PICKIN STRAWBERRIES,** *by Jenny Jackson, Gilbert, AZ. The titling type —a perfect finishing touch for this page—is cropped out of extra photographs taken during the strawberry-picking expedition.*

▲ **RAIN OR SHINE,** *by Deanna Lambson, Sandy, UT. Title letters cut from one of the background colored papers tie this layout together.*

◀ **BEAUTY,** *by Jamie Waters, South Pasadena, CA. A brief message, a stunning photograph, and delicate title letters contribute to a balanced page.*

way, you won't have to worry about staying in the lines.) Or use letter stickers to highlight the important words in your handwritten or computer-printed journaling.

To add a hint of extra color to a letter or word, rub colored chalk onto the sticker with a cotton swab, cotton ball, or your finger. To add a little extra dimension, outline each sticker with a medium-tipped marker or trim the edges with decorative scissors. You can also color a series of letter stickers with the same- or different-colored pencils or try creating patterns—plaids, squiggles, dots, among others—with felt-tip or metallic marker pens.

Add a little "punch" to your title by gluing small punched shapes to the letters. Or, for a fun effect, randomly punch through each letter and then place them on a colored background, allowing the complementary color to show through. Shaped stickers and fancy border stickers are another terrific way to make the most of your lettering.

▶ **ZENO FAMILY,** *by Melissa Zeno, Westland, MI. A simple list of words about the personality of your subject is an effective journaling device.*

▼ **THE TRAVELS OF KEN CHAMPION,** *by Shauna Berglun-Immel, Beaverton, OR. For a handwritten look, print out your computer journaling on a white sheet of paper, then trace it onto vellum. The title letters are on individual tags stuck onto the page.*

▶ **GROWING BY LEAPS AND BOUNDS,** *by Karen Towery, Acworth, GA. Bright colors, silly frogs, and bouncy title lettering celebrate this milestone in a young life.*

I have discovered it.
What? **Eternity.**
It is the **sea**
Matched with the **sun.**

Arthur Rimbaud

Scripps / UCSD Oceanographic Pier, La Jolla CA ~ February 2003

Decorative Accents

Remember, the essential elements of any scrapbook page are the photographs and the story behind them. That's it. You really don't need anything else. Decorative elements aren't essential, and creating custom artwork is certainly not required. We all love to drool over inspiring and mind-expanding creativity, but if trying to produce it is painful, then you really need to take anther route.

Scrapbooking is supposed to be fun—and even relaxing! Rejoice in the fact that the industry introduces new and exciting products and page accents every day. Use them. They'll help make your job of compiling scrapbooks easier. If it's been a while since you simply used patterned paper as a backdrop for your pictures, or just two stickers from a sheet to enhance a layout, remind yourself how refreshing this simple approach can be.

Take the easy way out every now and then. Instead of hand-cutting, stitching, embossing, gluing, and curling craft wire, look for shortcuts. Substitute readily available supplies—like stickers, rubber stamps, decorative scissors, templates, patterned papers, punches, and marker pens—for those handmade accents that take so much time. Instead of stitching on a button, glue it on!

Stickers

Scrapbooking is quicker with stickers—and these pages prove it! Stickers will liven up your scrapbook pages and save you lots of time. Here are a few tips that will make a believer out of you.

Mounting a sticker on tags or small pieces of white or colored cardstock will emphasize the sticker and give your page a more polished look. Journaling boxes are another great place to anchor stickers. For variety, try placing stickers directly on other page elements, like ribbon or vellum envelopes.

Where the Path May Lead, *by Wendy Smedley, Bountiful, UT. Punch-outs are an easy way to get accents onto your pages without spending a lot of time and money. Cardstock, buttons, patterned papers, and punch-outs all support the theme and tone of the photos.*

It Is The Sea, *by Tami Davis, Silverdale, WA. Take inspiration from the world around you. Neutral colors are everywhere—especially in the sea, sand, and surf. Tami repeated these colors with her choice of papers and rivets.*

▲ **I Love Bugs,** *by Renee Senchyna, Sherwood Park, Alberta, Canada. Can pages get any easier than this? With an adorable subject, bordered paper, and stickers, this page creates an eye-pleasing account of an afternoon of fun.*

With stickers, borders have never been easier. And with so many sticker styles to choose from, the design possibilities are practically endless. And there's a bonus—there's little measuring or cutting involved. Many stickers are made to be used as borders. Or why not combine multiple stickers to create your own? Whether they're used as subtle accents or as frames for photos or entire pages, border stickers are versatile page enhancers.

To use border stickers on a photo mat, cut one side of the mat larger than the others and simply adhere the stickers. This simple touch lends the "outer space" zest. Draw attention to photos or journaling by allowing them to "hang out" on a vertical border, where they'll grab the attention of even the most undiscerning eye. A vertical border strip is a refreshing way to isolate a photo and journaling block.

Cut stickers apart while they're still on the sheet. That way, you can move them around the page as you decide where to place them. When journaling with stickers, try jumbling the letters instead of placing them in a straight line. This casual look is easy to create—no ruler necessary! To remove a sticker mistakenly adhered to a surface, just use adhesive remover.

▲ **FRIENDS,** *by Pam Talluto. This decorative accent delight—recording Christmas memories with a best friend—includes a creative title made from metal, alphabet templates, tags, a page pebble and twine, among other supplies.*

▶ **FAMILY,** *by Donna Downey, Huntersville, NC. The muted background allows for multiple layers of pattern and embellishments, adding depth to the page. Distressing some of the elements adds to the vintage feel.*

Rubber Stamps

Rubber stamps are among the most versatile products a scrapbooker can work with. You can change colors as fast as you can swap ink pads, and you can stamp on everything from vellum to fabric. Plus, you can mix and match stamps to create an array of different looks.

Rubber stamps are extremely versatile. If you pick basic shapes and designs, you can maximize your collection and use them for years. You can actually start with just one stamp and one color of ink. Get comfortable working with that and expand a little at a time. You'll be addicted soon enough! With a little creativity, you can just change ink colors and create entirely different layouts with the exact same stamp.

When buying stamp pads, remember there are two types of ink. Dye inks dry quickly on paper surfaces, but tend to bleed a bit on porous surfaces. Pigment inks take slightly longer to dry, but will leave crisp, clear lines. Colors in each type can be purchased individually or in coordinated sets.

Solid stamps create a solid impression that requires no additional coloring. Outline stamps create a detailed or well-defined outline that you can color with markers, pencils, or chalks. Shadow stamps create a subtle, shaded area that draws the eye. You can then layer other stamped images or accents over these "shadows."

Border and frame stamps create an image that can be filled in or embellished. Roller stamps create a repetitive design that you can roll directly onto the paper. Background stamps cover a large surface area, and you can use them to create detailed backgrounds, like maps, floral patterns, repetitive words, etc. You can use alphabet stamps to create titles, journaling, embellishments, and more—without having to rely on your own handwriting.

You can find rubber stamps in scrapbook and craft stores, as well as online. And stamps are easy to store and maintain—all they need for an optimum lifespan is a cool, dark storage place (preferably away from dust) and a wipe-down with a good stamp cleaner after each use.

Even if you're just starting out, or you have limited time and money to invest in scrapbooking, you can still have fun with rubber stamps. Pick up one or more basic stamps, a couple of ink pads, and you're off! When you're ready to branch out, share the wealth by stamping with friends. You'll expand your possibilities by sharing stamps and inks—and it's a great excuse to spend time together.

Punches

The beauty of craft punches is that you can get a perfect shape every time—the edges are clean and crisp, and you don't have to worry about using scissors to cut out the smallest details. And you can punch shapes in paper of any color or texture to create a variety of effects.

If you're interested in starting a punch collection, consider starting with five basic punch shapes: square, circle, heart, star, and flower. You'll find plenty of uses for these universal shapes. They come in a variety of sizes, allowing you to layer your punches to create unique page accents. Consider using the "negative" of a punch—the punched-out shape—as embellishments, too. Once you've discovered the fun you can have with these basic punches, you'll be ready for more!

Swirl punches are an easy way to add movement and visual interest. Swirls make great embellishments, background images, patterned paper, and more. Try interlacing punched swirl shapes to create abstract designs. Or add swirls to a cardstock background and then cut the background into a wavy or curved shape.

▲ **A TASTE OF WINTER,** *by Marnie Flores. Three metal snowflake accents, a red mat, and a single red punched snowflake punctuate the clean lines of a cold-winter-day page.*

► **HAPPINESS,** *by Amy Schultz. A daisy punch, eyelets, and ribbon provide just the right touch to this basically block-style page.*

Decorating Chalks

Decorating chalks are known for their ability to shade and blend colors to create a soft, pastel finish. You can also draw with chalks to animate whimsical pages with cartoon-like frivolity. A delicate application of chalk can transform the look of clip art, add a 1940s hand-tinted look to black-and-white photos, and enliven an embossed design.

Chalks are one of the easiest ways to add color and visual interest to a layout. Creating a variety of looks is as easy as changing the tool you use to apply it. You can find several items to apply chalk at your local scrapbook or craft store—even your neighborhood grocery store. A few favorites are eye-shadow applicators, cotton swabs, cosmetic sponges, and cotton balls.

Eye-shadow applicators and cotton swabs are perfect for filling in details in small spaces, such as clip art and template images. They also work well for adding highlights and shading to pieced designs. Treat the applicator like a crayon or colored pencil and simply color in the area you choose.

Apply the chalk to your tool of choice and rub the color onto the design in a small circular motion, applying more chalk as you see fit. For an interesting effect, try applying chalk to a page background with a cotton pad, and then write or draw in it with a chalk eraser.

Try sponging chalk through a template to create a softly colored decorative detail. Just position the template on your page, daub a cosmetic sponge with stamping ink, and sponge color over the template. Be sure to clean the template before sponging your next image. And if you're sponging images that are close together, let the first image dry before placing the template down again. This way, you won't drag ink between the designs.

No matter what your project, you'll get the best results if you do a test on a scrap piece of paper first. This way, you'll get just the right amount of chalk on your applicator before you apply it to your page. And remember to use a clean applicator when switching from one color of chalk to another. This will keep you from mixing colors and will ensure that your chalk stays clean.

PIGGIES, *by Amy Williams, Old Town, ME. Add color and visual interest to a layout by applying chalk. You could use a make-up sponge or a cotton ball to add a hint of color to torn cardstock edges. The soft-pink chalk edges here complement the adorable piggie costumes.*

Setting Eyelets

Scrapbookers love eyelets. Available in so many colors, shapes, and sizes, eyelets do double duty as fasteners and decorative accents. To work with eyelets, you'll need these basic tools: an eyelet, hole punch, eyelet setter, and a hammer.

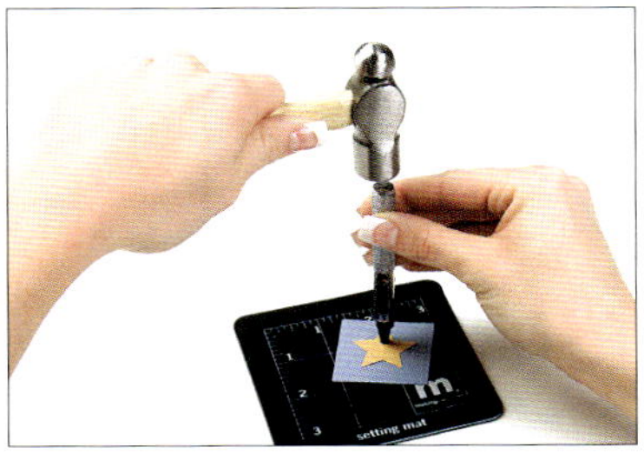

Step 1: *Start by deciding where you want the eyelet to go. Then punch a hole using the hole-punch tool, hammer, and setting mat.*

Step 2: *Turn the item over and place the eyelet in the hole, with the rough, long edge facing you.*

Step 3: *Place the eyelet setter in the middle of the eyelet and hammer until it's flattened.*

The finished eyelet.

Sample by Wendy Smedley.

▸ **MAGNETIC PERSONALITY,** *by Jamie Waters, South Pasadena, CA. Set off a black-and-white layout with a shock of bold color like the splash of red fiber and the two red eyelets decorating this dramatic page.*

Dry Embossing

What is dry embossing? It's a decorative art that uses paper, templates, and a stylus (or embossing tool) to literally raise the surface of your design from the paper. (Remember those fun, tactile relief maps and globes, with the mountainous regions of countries that jut up from the lowlands?)

To dry-emboss a design, tape a template with the design you want to a light box or hard surface. (A light box helps you view the template through the paper. If you don't have a light box, a sunny window works just as well; simply tape the template to your window.)

Choose which side of your paper you want the raised image to appear on, and place that side face down over the template. Trace only the outline of the design with the embossing tool. It's not necessary to "fill in" the interior area. The result? A beautiful raised image on your paper. (Make sure to turn your template backward if it contains letters.) Adding chalk to the dry-embossed image helps lift the design off the page and adds a hint of color. If necessary, soften the color by rubbing lightly with a second cotton swab or cotton ball.

Torn Paper

Torn paper adds great visual appeal to your scrapbook pages. You can tear paper in two ways: freeform and controlled. To create a freeform tear, lay your paper or cardstock on a flat surface. Grasp the top edge with the thumb and forefinger of one hand and slowly tear the paper toward you. Use the other hand to "guide" the tear as you go. Take your time, especially if you want to maintain a fairly straight and even tear. Keep pulling gently until the tear is complete.

The beauty of a freeform tear is that imperfection is perfectly okay. You're trying to achieve an organic, free-flowing edge on your cardstock. Don't worry if some of the torn area is wider or irregular—it just adds to the freeform look.

If you are a stickler for straight lines, try using the controlled-tear technique. Place a metal-edged ruler along the length of the paper you want to tear. Allow at least 1 inch of the paper to extend beyond the ruler so that you have something to grab onto. Press down on the ruler with one hand. With the other hand, rip the paper toward you with one motion, against the edge of the ruler.

Different kinds of papers will give you different results—so be sure to experiment. Cardstock is a heavier weight paper that is generally dyed all the way through, resulting in a torn edge that's the same color as the surface of the cardstock. When tearing vellum, you'll end up with a white line along the rough edge, similar to patterned paper. Consider chalking or inking the edges.

The pattern on patterned paper is often printed on white or light-colored paper, which means you'll have a white torn edge. This contrast may enhance or detract from your photos. If it detracts, you can easily dab a complementary color of ink or chalk along the white edge to soften it.

Mulberry and handmade papers generally contain long fibrous strands, making them a bit more difficult to tear. Dip a cotton swab in water and "paint" along the edge you'd like to tear to soften the fibers. You can also fold the paper along the tear line and simply lick the folded edge to dampen the paper.

Remember, paper has a grain. If the paper tears in a jagged edge, you may be tearing against the grain. If this is the case, turn your paper 90 degrees so you'll be tearing with the grain. If you're tearing a shape or wavy border, sketch the design with a pencil first, then tear the paper. If you're still having trouble, score the line you'd like to tear with a scoring blade (an option on some paper trimmers) or a stylus.

Create simple page accents by tearing with the freeform technique. Or try a controlled tear to create a particular shape—a box or a tag, for example—using an actual box or tag as a guide. You can use either technique, or even combine techniques, to create an attractive photo mat. Tear strips of paper to make a page background—or tear the edge of a photo to give the photo a unique or "antique" look.

SAND, *by Jamie Waters, South Pasadena, CA. Torn swirl patterned paper, vellum, and dark blue paper all contribute to the shoreline feel of this summertime page.*

▲ **A Random List of Things I Love,** *by Kim McCrary, Orem, UT. Journaled thoughts provide the impetus for this meaningful, personal scrapbook page with nine die-cut vellum envelopes containing photos and treasures galore.*

▲ **DADDY AND HIS LITTLE GIRL,** *by Kimberly Owens, Kihei, HI. Decorative accents for scrapbookers run a gamut beyond "soup to nuts." Here we have sand dollars, beads, and a wonderful torn-paper box to display vacation finds.*

Memorabilia Pockets

Memorabilia pockets are perfect for preserving seashells, coins, small photos, notes, dried flowers, tickets, and other trinkets that are otherwise difficult to include in a scrapbook. The self-adhesive, photo-safe, clear pockets come in a variety of sizes. (There's even one that holds a cassette tape so you can record your audio memories!)

Simply cut a square of colored paper that will fit inside the pocket to create a "background." Place your object or objects in the pocket. Seal the flap of the pocket, pull off the paper backing, and press it into place on your page.

▲ **MAX J. COULON,** *by Cynthia Coulon, Provo, UT. Stamping ink stains the edges of the tags and papers. The dark crackle paper amidst string, tags, stamps, and embossed stickers adds extra dimension to a basically simple page.*

Love Is What Binds Us Together, *by Nancy Yue, Baltimore, MD. A bold patterned ribbon is an effective contrast to a layout with otherwise muted tones.*

You Are My World, *by Margo Metzgar, Jonesboro, AR. The sea-blue patterned background paper echoes the theme of the layout with old maps and compass. The mesh netting and brads bring out the gold colors in the paper.*

Autumn Afternoon, *by Barbara Carroll, Tucson, AZ. Offsetting this photo in the bottom corner creates a strong visual appeal. The leaf motif is nicely echoed in the background paper and cut leaves.*

PALS
Kaden & Josh
Neighbors and Friends
4 Years old - July 2002

◂ **PALS,** *by Kimberly Fletcher, Vernal, UT. Bright patterned page-topper letters and colorful corner squares light up this page with an otherwise-neutral palate.*

▴ **McKENNA,** *by Stephanie McAtee, Kansas City, MO. This fabulous page is the perfect stage for an up-and-coming star! Soft-covered cardstock keeps the focus on the colorful photos. The decorative accents repeat those in the photos to great effect. Rose petals, tiny beads, and descriptive word strips complement the mood of the photographs.*

◂ **TIRE SWING,** *by Jenny Benge, Battle Ground, WA. Create the illusion of photo corners by attaching clusters of three eyelets or brads to opposite corners of a photo mat. For further interest Jenny continued the "chain" theme above the photo.*

▲ **My Sister's Birthday,** *by Annalia Romero, Silverdale, WA. Scraps of patterned paper and the easy imperfection of hand-drawn embellishments lend a festive feel to this birthday page.*

◀ **Cookie Love,** *by Marilyn Healey, Eagle Mountain, UT. Fiber, eyelets, and a vellum overlay add texture and interest to a sweet page.*

FUN

▲ **DOORWAYS IN STOCKDALE,** *by Lisa Russo, Woodstock, GA. Swirl shapes from the photograph are repeated in the title font and in the wire accents decorating the page.*

▶ **BLISS,** *by Amber Crosby, Houston, TX. Crop small details from photos and place them along the top of the page as a border. Rubber stamps, punches, eyelets, and vellum all contribute to the exuberance of the page.*

May 2003
Smile
My sweet Emily your smile melts my heart.

Digital Scrapbooking

Scrapbookers everywhere are turning to new high-tech methods of editing photos and working with text, creating realistic embellishments and inventing techniques that only a computer could create. Digital scrapbooking differs from traditional paper scrapbooking in more profound ways than just the replacement of paper with pixels. It draws heavily from graphic design concepts, featuring exact measurements and crisp lines. It makes color matching easier and more precise. It also allows scrapbookers to share layouts with friends thousands of miles away with a few clicks of the mouse. Yet, at its core, it has all the most important things in common with the paper scrapbooks we have been assembling for years.

Then e-mail the digital layouts to friends, post them on the Internet, print them out, save them on a CD-ROM—or start scrapbooking!

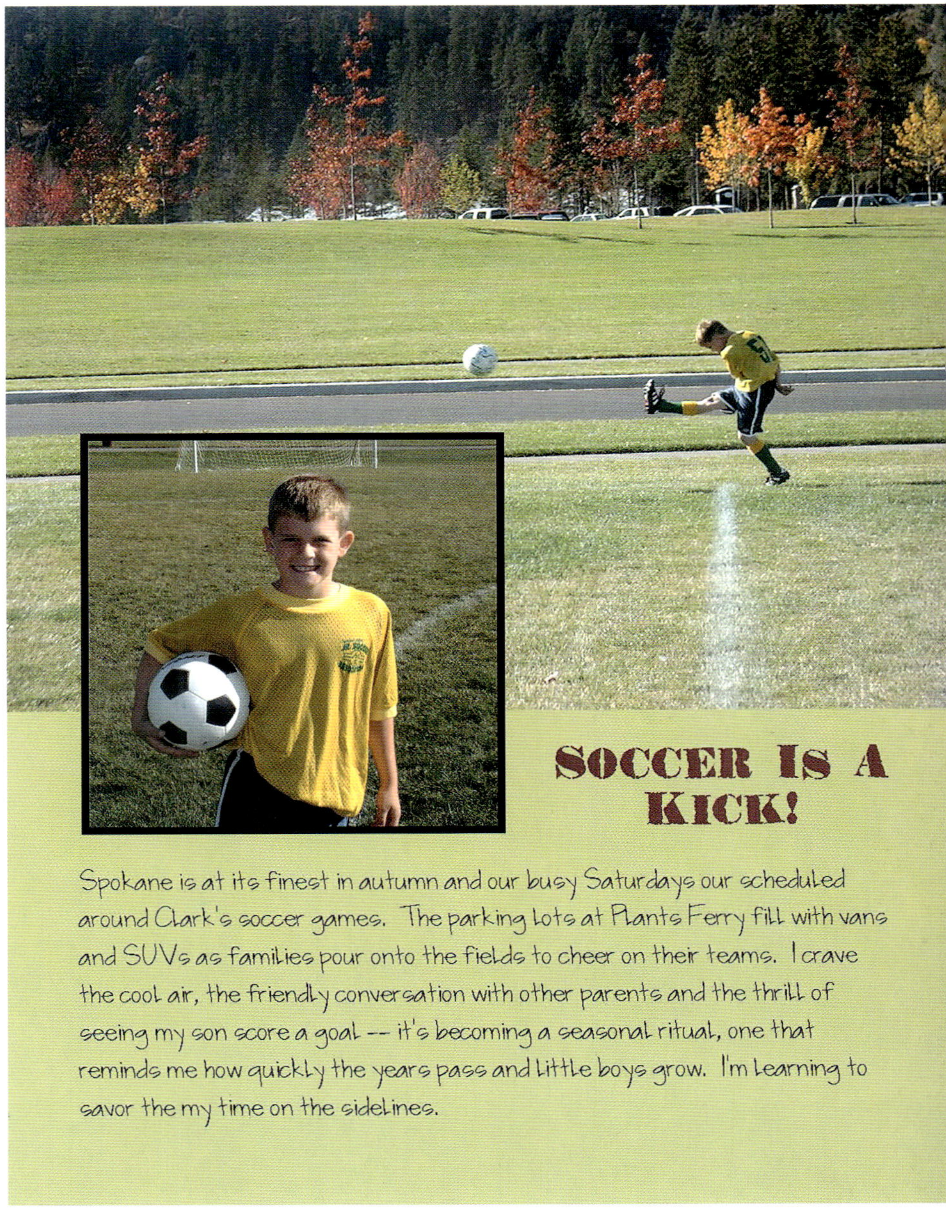

◄ **Smile,** *by Suzanne Flake, Tucson, AZ. A patterned band with colors drawn from Emily's dress includes touches of brown to balance the colored journaling panel and virtual fibers. Eyelets add a little zing as well.*

► **Soccer is a Kick,** *by Stacy Julian, Liberty Lake, WA. This digital page couldn't be any simpler or anymore clean cut. Using a larger background photograph and a smaller detail shot, plenty of space is left for recounting the Saturday game.*

Zenkoji Temple

In October 2001 I spent two weeks in Japan on business. On my day off, I traveled to Nagano via the Shinkansen to shop and tour the temple. Though the temple grounds were crowded and busy, there was a sense of peace and harmony. . While at the temple, I noticed a little girl being photographed by her family. I asked their permission to take her picture and her father smiled proudly and allowed me the privilege. This is my favorite photo from the trip...she is just beautiful and I love the traditional kimono paired with the pink and white sneakers.

On the top right is the Zenkoji Hondo, the main temple on the grounds and the largest temple in the region. Beneath the main hall, I walked in complete darkness on the path to Enlightenment, feeling the walls for the Key to Paradise. In the center photo, I'm turning a shantra believed to relieve personal pain and suffering. The bottom photo is of Buddhist prayer beads in the marketplace, just outside the gates of Zenkoji.

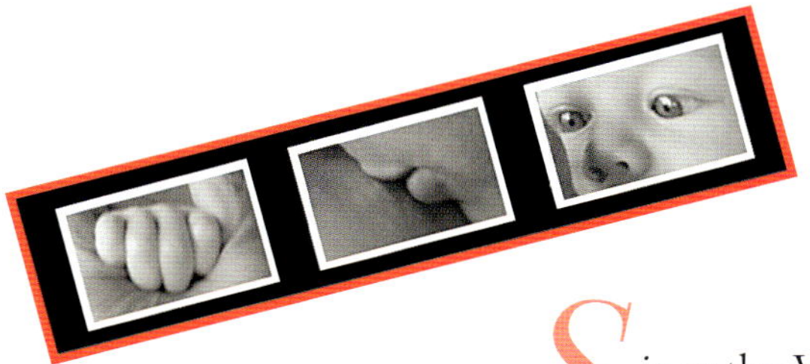

Digital Cameras

Since the Victorian era, scrapbookers have worked with paper, scissors, and glue. But digital scrapbooking requires a new set of equipment. Digital cameras, scanners, printers, and photo-editing software are the tools of the trade for computer scrapbookers. Here are a few of the benefits of working with digital image files:

INSTANT GRATIFICATION. With digital photography, you can see your shot in a matter of seconds, providing instantaneous assurance that you caught that once-in-a-lifetime moment.

SAVE MONEY. With digital image files, you only have to print the pictures you want. No more wasting money on poor prints.

EASY, SAFE STORAGE. Digital image files stored on a CD (Compact Disc) or DVD (Digital Versatile Disc) are less likely than negatives to be damaged when handled. Additionally, you can generally put 500 or more photographs on a CD.

NO FILM NEEDED. In a digital camera, memory cards replace film. Depending on the resolution of your camera, a 64MB (megabyte) memory card will hold at least 64 pictures. Delete poor photos immediately and reclaim the storage space. You can take photos all day and never have to reload.

SHARE PHOTOS CONVENIENTLY. Digital pictures can be shared with friends and family quickly via CD or e-mail. You can also print them out on your own printer. Many photo developers, including most large discount stores and self-serve photo kiosks, can make prints from your camera's storage device. Crop, add borders, change to black and white or sepia, remove red eye, and more. Your 4 x 6" or 5 x 7" photos can be printed and ready to go in less than an hour.

CREATE YOUR OWN BACKGROUNDS. Take a few shots of textures: bricks, grass, ripples in a pool. Use these photos as backgrounds for your digital scrapbook pages. After you're done shooting, load your photos into your computer in just a few simple steps.

◄ **ZENKOJI TEMPLE,** *by Teri Miner. A digital camera is an invaluable tool when you need to be sure you captured the moment, such as these pictures from Nagoro, Japan. This straightforward page includes Terri's favorite photo from the trip plus some background images. The stark red and black colors provide a stunning setting for a memorable day.*

▲ **FOCUS ON WHAT'S AHEAD,** *by Lisa Bieler, Los Angeles, CA. The three small detail photos are literally picked up from the focal-point photo, then saved and pasted into the white rectangles featured at the top of the page.*

Tips for Good Digital Design

When you first start creating layouts on your computer, the array of possibilities either seems endless or somewhat daunting. But have no fear! A solid understanding of good design is key to making your pages work.

Just because you can doesn't mean you should! Computer programs can do amazingly complex things, but when you're starting out, use restraint. Too many bells and whistles on a page can create chaos. Case in point: there is probably never going to be a reason to tint a picture of a child bright red. Too much digital intervention is sort of like "sticker sneeze" on a paper layout—you'll end up with something busy and overdone. Keep it simple to start and build from there.

KEEP THE EMPHASIS ON YOUR PHOTOS! They should be the primary focus of your layouts.

LIMIT YOURSELF TO NO MORE THAN TWO OR THREE FONTS ON A PAGE. Creating font harmony is easy if you keep it simple. Start by choosing a single font for both your title and journaling. Then, if you want more visual interest, choose a different font for your title. Often, one or two font styles on a page is just right. Too many fonts can definitely "spoil the soup."

RELY ON THE PRINCIPLES OF GOOD DESIGN. Repeating key embellishments, making thoughtful use of space, line, and shape, and creating balance on your page will all add up to a layout with harmony and flow. Go to your local library or bookstore and pick up a good, basic book on graphic design to help you build your skills as a page designer.

HAVE FUN! Once you start designing pages on your computer, you'll realize that anything is possible on a scrapbook page!

◄ **SMILES ARE THE SOUL'S KISSES,** *by Christine MacIlvaine, Oakland, NJ. Simple, yet powerful, this layout immediately draws attention to the beaming smiles of mother and daughter. Christine matted three small photographs on rectangles the same color as her border to create a seamless look.*

▲ **SAGUARO,** *by Suzanne Flake, Tucson, AZ. The Saguaro cactus flowers have a short life. They bloom at night and stay open for only one day. Suzanne really wanted the pictures to stand out, so she kept the layout simple and used a black background with white lettering.*

Using Digital Photos In Your Titles

1. Create a new blank image in your photo-editing software. The image used for this example was 8.5 x 11 inches in size, but you can create any size that fits your title. You can always copy and paste it into a layout later. Set the resolution to 300 dpi and the background to white.
2. Using the text tool, select a font with a block look.
3. Choose a large font size and type in your text.
4. Create a new layer. This layer will allow you to work on a new element in your design without altering the other items on your page.
5. Select the digital picture you want to use for the fill. Open the photo in a new window.
6. Use the Crop tool to frame the portion of the design you want to use. At this stage, pay more attention to the elements of the design than to the size of the area you're choosing. Once you're satisfied with your selection, crop the piece out.
7. Select your cropped piece and copy it. Close the window without saving changes. If you save at this stage, you'll replace your original photo with the cropped version.
8. Paste the cropped portion into your title image. Use the Move tool to position it over your text. If you like, rotate it into a different position.
9. Zoom in to view your image at 200% magnification. Set your Eraser tool to a larger diameter and roughly erase the photo around the letter you are filling. Switch to a small diameter to do the final, detailed erasing.
10. Because the text is not on the layer you are erasing, you can touch the line of each letter with the tool without spoiling the effect. However, if you erase inside the line and create a blank space inside the letter, use the Undo command to cancel your most recent action.
11. You can fill all the letters in your title with the same photo or you can use a different photo for each letter.
12. When you've filled each letter, use the Merge Layers or Flatten Image command to combine all your elements into one layer. Save your work, and you'll be ready to place your custom-made titled block anywhere you like in your layout.

▶ **MEANT TO BE,** *by Margie Lundy, Greenfield, OH. A few photos and some software will help create a layout as simple or busy as you wish.*

Some things were meant to be...

Chuck 1949

Josh 2001

like my grandpa and me.

After adopting our son from Ukraine, we couldn't believe how much Josh resembled my dad in these old photos. These two have such a special bond that it's clear they were meant to be together. Only God could reach across time and space to find such a perfect match.

▲ **NEMO,** *by Julie Hung, Pearland, TX. Tinting a black-and-white photo calls immediate attention to a focal point in the image. For this digital shot, Julie used Adobe Photoshop 7 to apply photo tinting to the goldfish.*

Photo-Editing Software

Photo-editing software is the connection between your digital photos and your digital scrapbook layouts. Once you've transferred your photos from your camera or scanner to your computer, these software packages allow you to do anything from fixing "red eye" to creating a layout complete with virtual vellum, tags, and fibers to adding color to black-and-white photos.

Think about the scrapbooking supplies you use most frequently—patterned papers with subtle washes of color, lacy-textured fibers, eyelets and brads in every shape and size. With photo-editing software, you can now recreate the look of these favorites without ever touching scissors or paper. You can also experiment with sleek contemporary effects you can't duplicate with conventional scrapbooking tools.

There are many types of software that will suit a scrapbooker's needs. The best of them offer a similar set of core features. Color correction, multiple layers for creating complex images, and the ability to add and reshape text are some of the functions most frequently used. Crop, marquee, and fill tools and "Move," "Rotate," and "Zoom" commands are just some of the additional options. Familiarize yourself with the specific features available with your software program.

Scanners

Scanners work like copying machines. You can scan anything that will lie flat—from heirloom photographs to swatches of fabric. Many scanners have one-touch copying functions, which allow you to scan and print an item in a single step.

You'll appreciate the way a scanner lets you make a flat, scrapbook-safe version of items you might otherwise find too bulky, sharp, or abrasive to place in an album. Create an eye-catching collage without the added bulk or the messy glue. And scanned copies of photos give you much more freedom to experiment with techniques (such as changing color, tinting, or even "tearing" the edges of photos) that you wouldn't think of trying with your precious original photographs.

There are many creative possibilities when working with a scanner. Scan your paper scrapbook pages, then burn them onto a CD, post them on the Internet, or e-mail them to a friend. Scan a collection of items that give the details of your family's everyday life—school papers, shopping lists, energy bills—and incorporate them into a layout. Paper clips, crocheted doilies, interesting pebbles from the front yard—if they'll fit on the bed of your scanner, you can add them to a layout! If an item is so bulky that your scanner's lid won't close over it, drape the scanner with a towel to keep light from leaking in around the edges as you scan. Be careful when placing rough items on the scanner so you don't scratch the glass. Scan representative artwork from your child's (or your own!) early years and reduce the images so that you can fit several onto a single layout. Scan pages from old books, photos from outdated calendars, even carpet samples.

Digital Details

When you scrapbook with your computer, getting an exact match is as easy as clicking on a color in your photo and then clicking on a page element. Use the eyedropper tool to pick up photo colors and duplicate them in the layout. You have every color of "paper" available to you at any time. And even better, it doesn't cost anything to experiment and practice. There is no actual photo, paper, or cardstock to ruin. If you aren't happy with your layout, keep changing it until you are.

Don't have just the right patterned paper? Create a perfect match with colors taken right from your photos. Or design your own patterned papers in coordinating colors and textures. Pick elements from your photos to repeat elsewhere on your layout for tailor-made embellishments. Design your own "rubber stamp" images. With digital scrapbooking, you can add as many elements as you like and still be free to move or remove them later.

◀ **EVOCATIVE,** *by Amy Sorensen. Combining the old with the new is an excellent way to capture all your memories without the painstaking process of handwriting all of your journaling. The computer-generated journaling provides a clean, strong support for the three photos*

▶**THE COURTSHIP OF PHILIP AND AGNES,** *by Michelle Shefveland. Design your own patterned papers in coordinating colors and textures.*

The Courtship of Philip and Agnes

Grandpa and Grandma walking along a beach? What an uncommon site for two small town Minnesota farm kids in 1927. When I dug into the story, it turns out they were just at a lake near their home during their courtship. They look like they are movie stars from Hollywood!

If Roses Grow In Heaven

If roses grow in Heaven,
Lord please pick a bunch for me,
Place them in my Mother's arms
And tell her they're from me.
Tell her that I love her and miss her,
And when she turns to smile,
Place a kiss upon her cheek
And hold her for awhile.
Because remembering her is easy,
I do it every day,
But there's an ache within my heart
Because I am missing her today.

AUG 27 2003

Titles and Journaling

A title sets the mood for your entire page. When choosing a style for your title, select one that conveys the emotion of the layout, but make sure it's easy to read. The more complex the font you choose, the shorter your title should be.

Script typefaces are exactly as they sound: script or cursive style. From the very elaborate to the highly stylized, script faces are perfect for adding extra elegance or drama to a page title. Display, or decorative, type incorporates everything in the type world that's fun and unique. You'll find a typeface for almost every mood or theme you can dream up!

When it comes to choosing fonts for journaling, keep it simple. Funky fonts may work for titles, but they're not the best option for journaling blocks. Does this mean you can't have any fun with fonts? Absolutely not! Just start out simple, gain some type confidence, and then begin to experiment. You want your journaling to be readable and not distract from the overall feel of the layout. Be sure to make your type at least nine points in size.

Serif typesfaces, such as Times, Garamond, and Goudy, have thick and thin strokes in their letterforms. In general, serif typefaces are the easiest to read.

Sans serif typefaces, such as Arial, Helvetica, and Gill Sans, have uniform widths in their letterforms, with no thin or thick strokes. Sans serif typefaces are clean and modern in appearance, and tend to feel more informal and friendly. Sans serif fonts work well for information that you want to stand out on the page.

▶ **HOME, HEARTS, AND HANDS,** *by Patti Jewkes, Sandy, UT. These lively titles were printed on vellum from computer fonts. The simple designs add elegance and variety without a lot of work or money.*

▶ **WELCOME HOME, BABY,** *by Joannie McBride, Herriman, UT. With computer fonts, you can create timeless titles and journaling in a snap.*

◀ **IF ROSES GROW IN HEAVEN,** *by Tami Davis, Silverdale, WA. Find a favorite photo of your mother and pay tribute to her on a scrapbook page. Whether it's rocky or rosy, the mother-daughter relationship is one to acknowledge, learn from, and celebrate. By using computer fonts and fonts downloaded from the Internet, you can easily create beautiful journaling. Tami embellished the page with simple flowers.*

Printing Your Pages

Printers make the connection between your virtual and physical scrapbook pages. You can print the images you've scanned or taken with your digital camera for your paper scrapbook pages. You can also print out the titles and journaling blocks you've created with computer fonts. But you also need a printer to output your digital scrapbook pages if you want to include them in an album or display them anywhere other than on a computer.

For most scrapbookers, inkjet printers are an inexpensive, easy-to-use choice. Several models of large-format printers are now available at prices within the reach of the average scrapbooker, offering high-quality image reproduction and the capability to print on papers up to 14 inches wide. Before tucking your printed layouts into a page protector, however, allow them to dry overnight. This is especially important if you are printing on glossy paper, which can easily smudge if not handled properly.

Safe and Secure

After you've gone through all the work of creating your layouts, you'll want to make sure they'll be safe for future generations to enjoy. A CD-ROM (Computer Disc-Read Only Memory) provides an excellent way to archive your digital photos and your digital scrapbook pages. Many new computers have CD recorders, and low-cost external recorders are available for older machines. Most photo developers can also create CD-ROMs.

CD-ROMS offer a number of advantages over other storage systems. They're waterproof, scratch resistant, small enough to rest in the palm of your hand, and able to hold copies of dozens of high-resolution digital layouts. They're also inexpensive, easy to mail or store, and readable by any computer. You can make one copy of your album to send to faraway family members and another to keep for yourself.

It's also a good idea to copy your digital photos and layouts—at least the most important ones to CD and store the discs at a location other than your home, in case of fire, flood, or other natural disaster. If your originals should be lost, you'll be able to print new copies from your CDs. Some scrapbookers even scan their paper layouts and save them on CD so that if anything should happen to the precious originals, they'll always be able to recreate their work.

▸ **MEETING FACE TO FACE,** *by Gina Cabrera, Phoenix, AZ. Simple, unadorned photos dominate this straightforward page. Decorative accents are used in colors pulled right from the photo.*

meeting
face to face

Meeting the bottlenose dolphins was the one event you were looking forward to Zac. You were thrilled to see and touch them as they swam up to us for a visit. They were smooth to the touch, very friendly and quite talkative. Their beauty, grace and charm were captivating. This is one of many favorite photos that will bring back wonderful memories.

San '03 Diego

SEA WORLD SEA WORLD SEA WORLD SEA WORLD SEA WORLD SEA WORLD SEA WORLD SEA WORLD SEA WORLD SEA

AIRBORNE, *by Sharon Whitehead, Vernon, British Columbia, Canada. These fabulous bright-colored balloons certainly create rhythm and motion as they float across the spread.*

RE/MAX

◀ **ONE SNOWY DAY,** *by Robin Johnson, UT. The journaling—simple in concept and in style—is printed out from the computer and mounted onto decorative tags.*

▶ **MY SWEET MIRIAM,** *by Kim Morgan. The softness of the pleated vellum is reinforced by the delicate italic typeface printed on torn vellum paper.*

▶ **MOMENTS,** *by Cheryl Overton, Kelowna, BC, Canada. Type downloaded from the internet and software to convert the picture to sepia helped in the creation of this graceful scrapbook page.*

Moments
moments
life is lived in moments
savor the memories
and the joys they offer
life

Tuesday

It's all in a day's

To enjoy our work, and feel that it is worthwhile, what more c

Nancy's log

8am- Arrive at the MRI center; review cases sent by my colleagues for second opinions, and call them back to discuss the cases.

8:30- Read the MRI scans from the previous evening. There are scans depicting a new stroke, an abnormal blood vessel in the brain, a spinal fracture, and cancerous metastases. Discuss patients' results with several physicians and answer their questions about MRI.

12pm- Realize how far behind I am, sigh, and decide to skip lunch. I find a case of multiple sclerosis, a cervical syrinx (hole in the spinal cord), a brain infection, and the usual smattering of degenerative spine disease and disc herniations.

2:30- Finally finished the first batch, and getting hungry. A partner calls from another hospital for a consult on a neck case; I can review it on our teleradiology system.

3:00- The chief MRI technologist comes to discuss next year's MRI needs for the practice. Two new MRI scanners are planned at other sites, and major upgrades at two other locations. Estimated costs- $5.5 million. We need to prioritize these needs and discuss them with the MRI committee members. My nanny calls to discuss choice of soaps for my youngest, who has multiple allergies and eczema. She updates me on the children.

3:15- The day's scans on the hospital inpatients arrive in a clump. These patients are quite ill, and I discuss the cases with the neurologists and neurosurgeons. Another case is sent on tele-radiology by a partner in my practice, showing a herpes infection of the brain.

3:30- I take time to meet with a surgeon about his own MRI results. Michael (my 12 year old) calls to ask how to start the DVD player at home. I get back to my desk, and read scans without taking a break. By the time I finish at 5:10, I have looked at over six thousand images on around fifty patients.

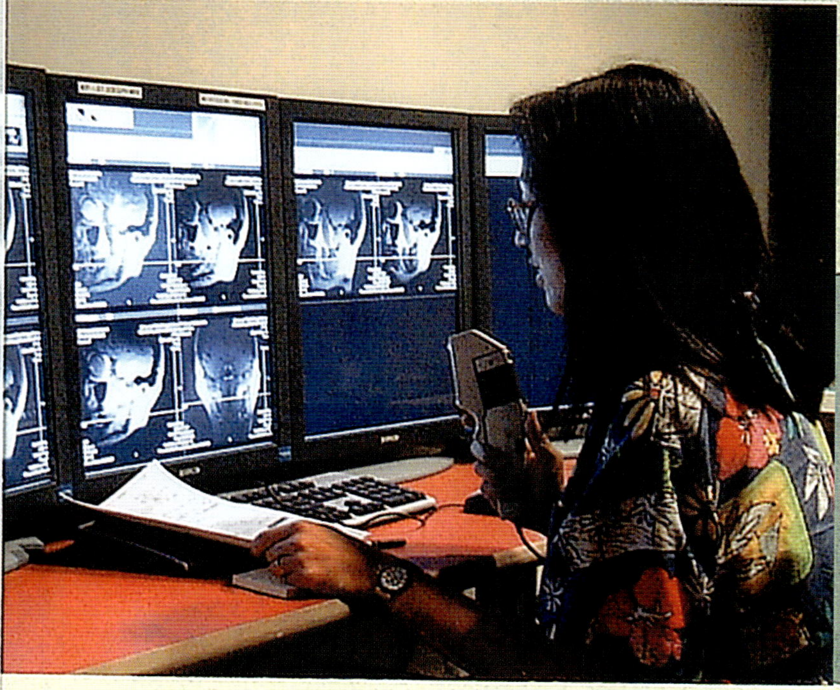

Neuroradiologist & Medical Director

The privilege of discovery

Every so often, the veil of confusing experimental results is parted, and something deep and beautiful about how biological life works is revealed. It is as if a syllable that God spoke becomes suddenly audible. The thrill of unearthing such 'God speak' is one of the special rewards of my profession.

The joy c scientific

with stude side. Sci research inv and writi sparsely punc moments of su engaging in su as a team, wi that become builds a spe enduring b become marke that elevate

David speaks o of being a medi

Hopkins Medical Prof

Why do I (Nancy) enjoy my work?

I am always learning

In my field, technology drives advances rapidly. I am always learning new techniques and tools; otherwise, my skills would become obsolete.

I am never bored

Every patient is unique, and so is their expression of disease. Every scan is like a small package of mysteries to be revealed to the intrepid sleuth.

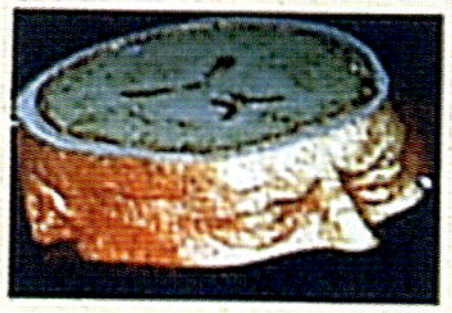

I can make a difference

My colleagues send me complex cases daily for an expert opinion. I am happy when I can make an accurate diagnosis in a difficult case and help the doctors treating their patients.

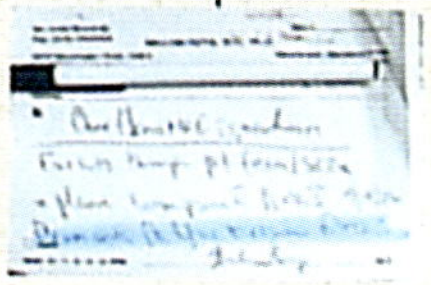

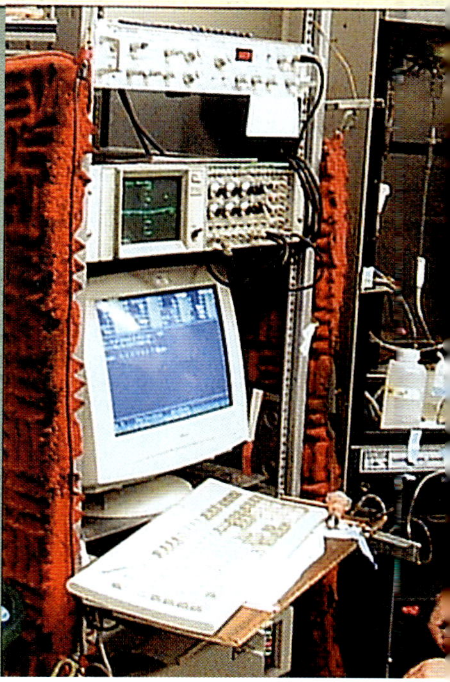

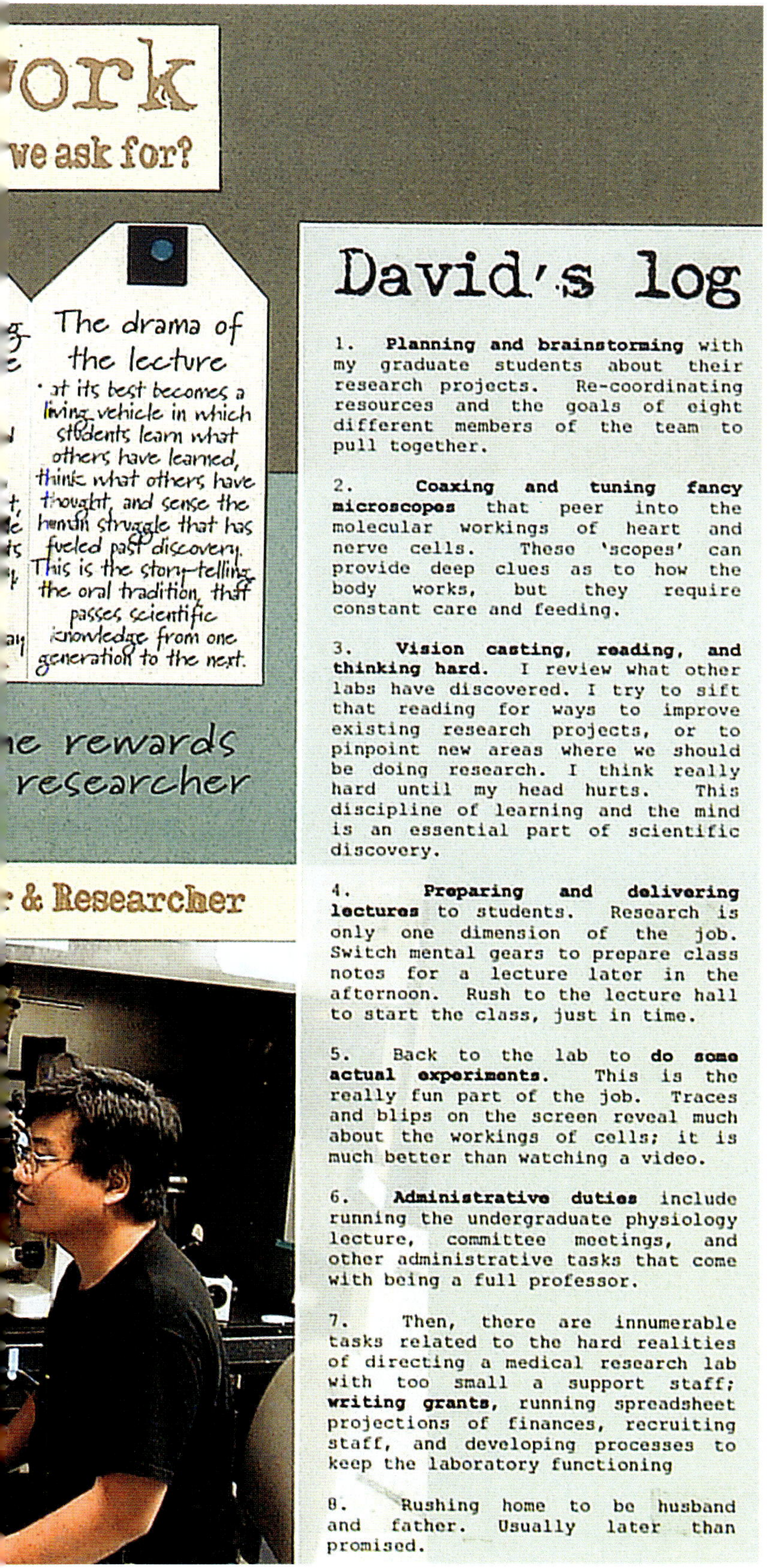

CELEBRATING THE EVERYDAY MOMENTS, *by Nancy Yue, Baltimore, MD. Using a digital camera, photo-editing software, the newest clip art images, and clean colorblocking, Nancy created this state-of-the-art album. The warm, inviting pages rival the handmade look. Not only do the clip-art bookplates and tags look "real," but each page features prolific and poignant journaling, giving incredible insight into Nancy's life.*

Source Guide

Page 3: **Giggle**
Patterned paper (Mustard Moon and Making Memories); ink (Clearsnap, Inc.); Butterbrotpapier font (Internet).

Page 6: **Yankee Doodle Daniel**
Star punch (McGill); star buttons (Dress It Up); Doodle Cursive font (Cock-a-Doodle Designs, Inc.); pop dots (Close To My Heart); Foam mounting tape (3M).

Page 7: **Freedom**
Flower stamp (Close to My Heart); ink (Stampin'Up!); photo corners and Simply Stated Rub-ons (Making Memories); ZIG Millenium pen (EK Success)

Pages 8 & 9: **My Life, 2004**
Materials: metal album (ScrapWorks); pattern papers (SEI); metal letters (Making Memories); alphabet stamps (Hero Arts)rub-ons (Craf-T Products)

Page 11: **My Eyes Are an Ocean**
Vellum (Paper Pizazz); letter stickers (Colorbök); poem (twopeasinabucket.com); seashell

Page 12: **Baby's Faces**
Patterned paper and tags (SEI); Sonnets patterned paper (Creative Imaginations); Baby Kruffy title font and Angelica journaling font (Internet).

Page 13: **Esther and Edwin**
Patterned paper, frame, border, page accents (K & Company); tags (Provo Craft); chalk (Craf-T Products); eyelets (Creative Impressions); Doodle Cursive font (Cock-A-Doodle Design, Inc.); twine.

Page 17: **Christmas Morning**
Textured paper (Provo Craft); snowflake brads (Making Memories); Poor Richard font (Microsoft Word); embroidery floss; brads.

Page 18: **Emily & Ben**
Patterned paper (C-Thru Ruler Co.); Scriptina title font (Internet); CK Flourish journaling font (*Creating Keepsakes*); vellum; chalk; brads.

Page 19: **Happy 90th Birthday!**
Patterned paper (Colors By Design); photo corners (3L Corp.); Sticko number sticker (EK Success); Bickley Script font (Internet).

Page 21: **Letters from Mom to My Girls**
Floral paper (Colors By Design); striped paper (Keeping Memories Alive); dark brown paper (Frances Meyer); light brown paper (Carolee's Creations); tags (Making Memories); fibers (On the Surface); Zig Writer pen (EK Success).

Page 22: **Autumn Beauty**
Slick Writer pen (American Crafts); letter charm (Making Memories).

Page 22: **Coming Full Circle**
Patterned paper (Scrap-Ease); Fonts: CK Cursive (title) and CK Bella (journaling). *The Best of Creative Lettering* CD Vol. 2 and 3; leaf (Nature's Pressed).

Page 23: **Fish All Day**
Leere, "Family Frenzy" Computer font (HugWare CD, Provo Craft); stickers (Provo Craft); antique brads.

Page 24: **Smile**
Patterned paper (Karen Foster Design and Making Memories); eyelets and metal word (Making Memories); photo corners (EK Success); ribbon.

Page 25: **It's Not About What You Catch**
Mini-brads (American Pin & Fastener); Anandale mono font for title and subhead; Adobe Garamond for journaling (Adobe Systems); enhanced photo paper (Epson).

Page 26: **Thank You**
1942 Report font (Internet); patterned paper (7 Gypsies); paper flowers; walnut ink (Post Modern Design).

Page 27: **Cold Lips, Warm Hearts**
Alphabet stamps (PSX); fibers (Fibers by the Yard); tags (Avery Dennison); eyelets; alphabet beads (The Beadery); wire.

Page 28: **Feelin' Frosty**
Page enhancements (Cock-A-Doodle Design, Inc.); "sponge" paper (Paper Adventures); embroidery floss (DMC); Doodle Basic Computer font (*Page Printables* CD, Cock-A-Doodle Design, Inc.).

Page 29: **Hilary Harker**
Patterned paper (Paper Garden, Doodlebug Designs, Inc., and All My Memories); letter stickers (SEI); square metal-rimmed tag (Making Memories).

Page 30: **Winter Schminter**
Patterned paper (Jennifer Collection and Wordsworth); Sailboat and Submarine fonts (twopeasinabucket.com); Monet font (P22 Type Foundry); Falling Snowflakes font (GalloFonts).

Page 31: **Marinne Turns 3**
Patterned paper (Colors By Design); Zig Writer pen (EK Success); CK Journaling and CK Groovy computer fonts (*The Best of Creative Lettering* CD Vol. 2, *Creating Keepsakes*).

Page 32: **Mother and Son**
Angelica computer font, Black Boys on Mopeds journaling font, and Mandingo font (Internet); stars (homemade design).

Page 33: **Grandpa Doug**
Apple Harvest Scrap Pad patterned paper, PC Ratatat font; brads (Provo Craft); rubber stamps (PSX); die cuts (Sizzix); label maker (Dymo); stamping ink (Close to My Heart).

Page 33: **How Is It Possible?**
Patterned paper (Debbie Mumm); Arial and Gift fonts (twopeasinabucket.com).

Pages 34-35: **All Star Kids**
Patterned paper (Northern Spy); die-cut block letters (My Mind's Eye); Zig Writer pen (EK Success); CK Fun computer font (*The Art of Creative Lettering* CD, *Creating Keepsakes*); oval template (Provo Craft).

Page 36: **Blowing Bubbles**
Patterned paper and stickers (Karen Foster Design); Bambino font (Internet).

Page 37: **Homemade Teddy Bears**
Patterned paper (All About Me Paper Co. and The Paper Patch); eyelets (Prym-Dritz); CK Newsprint and CK Journaling fonts (*Creating Keepsakes*); tags; fibers; embroidery floss.

Page 38: **Sand**
Century Gothic font (Microsoft Word); Trubble font (Internet).
Page 39: **Ballerina**

Page 39: **Ballerina**
Patterned paper (Magenta); vellum (Paper Pizazz); Scriptina font (Internet); pop dots (All Night Media); rhinestones.

Pages 40-41: **Shell Seekers**
Sonnets shell stickers (Creative Imaginations); Arial font (Microsoft Word); fiber, watch crystals; seashells.

Page 42: **A Season of Change**
Patterned paper (All My Memories); stickers (me and my BIG ideas); Chestnut font (twopeasinabucket.com); rub on words and phrase (Making Memories); eyelets.

Page 43: **Blowing Bubbles**
Patterned paper (Doodlebug Design, Inc); page pebbles and date stamp (Making Memories); slide (KI Memories); Hooked on Booze font (Internet); metal circles; ribbon; transparency; poem by Thena Smith.

Page 44: **Color of Your Heart**
Specialty paper (Magic Scraps); title templates (Deja Views, Wordsworth, Hero Arts); journaling (PSX); Zig Writer pen (EK Success); chalk.

Page 45: **Peek**
Renae Lindgren paper, stickers, and borders (Creative Imaginations); CK Handprint font (*Creating Keepsakes*).

Page 47: **Soak Up the Sun**
Stickers (SEI); buttons (Making Memories); brads (Karen Foster Designs); net (Magenta); tag (Hot Off the Press).

Page 48: **On the Ice**
Eyelets (Making Memories).

Page 48: **Times I Treasure**
Alphabet titles (Making Memories); metal word (Creative Imaginations); Zig Writer pen (EK Success).

Page 49: **Jemma's Sunflowers**
CK Script computer font (*The Best of Creative Lettering* CD Vol.1, *Creating Keepsakes*); Scriptina (Internet); fibers (Rub-A-Dub Dub); rubber stamps (Hero Arts); Stamping ink (VersaMark, Tsukineko); sunflower.

Page 50: **Adventure in Arches, 2002**
Brush Script font; square punch (Emagination Crafts, Inc.).

Page 51: **Colors of the Sea**
Zig Writer pen (EK Success).

Page 52: **A Perfect Golden Afternoon**
Dolphin, Corel computer fonts; die cut (Heartland Paper Co.).

Page 54: **Zack and Jake**
Stamps (PSX); ink (Clearsnap, Inc.); metal-rimmed tags and brads (Making Memories); chalk; fibers.

Page 55: **Joy**
Holly stickers and Crystal Accents (Mrs. Grossman's); ribbons (Close To My Heart); letter stickers (Doodlebug Designs); green tag (Making Memories); black pen.

Page 55: **Snow**
Charms (Making Memories); chalk; CK Journaling and CK Cursive fonts (*Creating Keepsakes*); floss.

Page 56: **The Joy of Discovery**
Girls Are Weird computer font (Internet); daisy and leaf punches (Family Treasures); eyelets (Impress Rubber Stamps); vellum (Paper Garden).

Page 57: **Gardens**
Patterned paper (NRN Designs); daisy accent (Kangaroo and Joey); Edwardian Script title font (Internet); Times New Roman journaling font (Microsoft Word); circle punches (Family Treasures, Inc. and Marvy Uchida); ribbon charm and vellum tag (Making Memories).

Page 57: **Remember This**
Patterned paper and tags (Rusty Pickle); eyelets, metal letters, and rub-on (Making Memories); Zig Writer pen (EK Success); photo corners (Xyron Gold).

Page 57: **What a Silly Face!**
Patterned paper (Making Memories); stickers (Provo Craft); computer font (Doodle Tipsy, *Page Printables* CD Vol. 1, Cock-A-Doodle Design, Inc.).

Page 58: **Myrtle Beach, 2002**
Garamouche font (P22 Type Foundry); Jolee's Boutique stickers (Stickopotamus); tag (Avery); embroidery floss (DMC); pop dots (All Night Media).

Page 58: **Memory**
Zig Writer pen (EK Success); charms; fibers.

Page 59: **I'll Go In If You Do**
Submarine punch (The Punch Bunch); animal cutouts (Basic Bear Designs); raffia.

Page 60: **Be Yourself**
Rub-on words (Making Memories); MA Sexy and Marydale fonts (Internet).

Page 61: **A Cowboy Kiss**
Acrylic paint (Plaid); die-cut (KI Memories); embossing powder (Ranger Industries, Inc.); Texas Hero and Teletype fonts (Internet).

Page 62: **Nate**
Patterned paper, square frame and tag (Chatterbox, Inc,); letter tiles (Westrim Crafts); stickers (Pebbles, Inc., Memories Complete and Creative Imaginations); Zig Writer pen (EK Success).

Page 63: **Glimpses of Christmas**
CK Script font (*Creating Keepsakes*).

Pages 64-65: **Nothing Sweeter**
Skeleton leaves (Club Scrap); square punch (Marvy Uchida); ribbon (Stampin' Up!).

Page 66: **She Loves Me**
Patterned paper and letter stickers (Chatterbox, Inc.); stickers (Mrs. Grossman's); marker (EK Success).

Page 67: **Glee**
Left: Page accents (Paper Fever); mesh (Magic Mesh); glitter (Magic Scraps); slide holders.
Right: Cardstock (Canson); stickers (StickyPix, Paper House Productions); Zig Millennium pen (EK Success).

Page 68: **Endless Summer**
Fresh Cuts page accents (EK Success); tags (Making Memories); Yippy Skippy font (Internet); chalk (Craf-T Products); Page pebble (Making Memories).

Page 69: **Sisters**
Patterned paper and rivets (Chatterbox); Newsprint font (*Creating Keepsakes*); vellum.

Page 70: **Expressive**
Zig Writer pen (EK Success); embroidery floss.

Pages 70-71: **A Colonial Independence**
Patterned paper (Ever After Scrapbook Co.); star punch (Family Treasures); Nuptial Script computer font (Adobe); scanned replica of the Declaration of Independence.

Page 71: **Trimming the Tree**
Ribbon (Offray); vellum tag (Making Memories); embroidery floss; Carpenter and Evergreen fonts (twopeasinabucket.com).

Page 72: **Sparkle**
Circle tags (Making Memories); Jolee's Boutique snowflake stickers (EK Success); circle punches (Emagination Crafts, Inc.); vellum.

Page 72: **Only Time Will Tell**
Patterned paper (Rusty Pickle, Chatterbox, Inc. and 7 Gypsies); page pebble (Make Memories); die cuts (KI Memories); stamps (Wordsworth); ink (Clearsnap, Inc.); stickers (Chatterbox, Inc.); ribbon; watch crystal.

Page 73: **Brush Your Teeth**
Patterned paper (Two Busy Moms); pen (Zig Memory Systems, EK Success); brads (Boxer Productions); mesh (Magic Mesh).

Page 73: **Sometimes It's the Smallish Things**
Button (Jesse James & Co., Inc.); Garamouche font (Internet); Twistel (Making Memories); chalk (Craft-T Products).

Page 74: **Snow Days**
Letter stickers (My Mind's Eye); pop dots (All Night Media); Zig Writer pen (EK Success); snowflake punch (Westrim Crafts).

Page 75: **Ten Things**
Patterned paper (EK Success); Fresh Cuts page accents (EK Success); tags (Angelia's own designs); eyelets (Making Memories); chalk (Craf-T Products); Zig Writer pens (EK Success); Garamouche font (Internet).

Page 76: **The Man Behind the Daddy**
Patterned paper (7 Gypsies and Anna Griffin); letter stickers (Doodlebug Design, Inc. and Wordsworth); Jolee's by You flower stickers (EK Success); Garamouche font (P22 Type Foundry); square punch (Marvy Uchida); Sonnets wax seal (Creative Imaginations); gingham ribbon.

Page 77: **Infinite Possibility**
Letter stickers (Brenda Walton, K & Company); wild flower and tree stickers (Provo Craft); Kayleigh computer font (Internet).

Page 77: **Dip, Hop, Jump**
Circle and square patterned paper (Paper Fever); light-blue and white patterned paper (Provo Craft); aqua patterend paper (Stamping Station); metal tags and buttons (Making Memories); alphabet rubber stamps (Hero Arts); metallic eyelets (Simple Ideas); brads (Karen Foster Design); embossing powder; stamping ink (Tsukineko).-

Page 78: **Blades of Grass**
Patterned paper (Sonburn); Avant Garde and Roger's Typewriter fonts (Internet); Pop Dots (Therm O Web); rickrack; flower cut from patterned paper.

Page 79: **Ryanspeak**
Zig Writer and Zig Millennium pens (EK Success); craft wire (Artistic Wire Ltd.); star (homemade design).

Page 80: **Favorite Things**
Vellum (Paper Accents); metal tag (Avery); shopping bag and music note stickers (Mrs. Grossman's); pencil jar and bubble bath stickers (Colorbök); vintage shoe, nail polish, antique horse and dragonfly stickers (Frances Meyer); heart sticker (me & my BIG ideas); cocoa, cake, sand pail, poinsettia and ladybug stickers (Susan Branch); lipstick sticker (WhipperSnapper Designs); orchid sticker (Sandylion); baby foot rubber stamp (Hero Arts); key and kite rubber stamps (Close To My Heart); stamping ink; Adorable, Antique, Architect, Ariel, Biffo, Bookworm, Boys R Gross, Cartoon, Cezanne and Yippy Skippy fonts (Internet); CK Journaling, CK Handprint, CK Wired, CK Chemistry and CK Constitution fonts (*Creating Keepsakes*); Arizona font (twopeasinabucket.com); KF Dimple font (Karen foster Design); LD Mixed font (Inspire Graphics); craft wire (Artistic Wire Ltd.); mini-brads (American Pin & Fastener).

Page 81: **Dear Santa**
Patterned paper (Autumn Leaves); black patterned paper (7 Gypsies); Soli and First Grade font (Internet).

Page 82: **In the Morning**
Zig Writer pen (EK Success); brads.

Page 82: **I Love Your Smile**
Vellum tags, eyelets and snowflake charm (Making Memories); Sticko letter stickers (EK Success); buttons; vellum.

Page 83: **The Way to Know Life**
Quote sticker (WordsWorth); snaps (Making Memories).

Page 84: **Son, Brother, Friend**
Papyrus computer font (Microsoft Word).

Page 85: **Pickin Strawberries**
CK Script font (*Creating Keepsakes*); Watermelon lettering template (ScrapPagerz); Puff Paint (Delta).

Page 86: **Rain or Shine**
Stickers (Magenta and Pebbles, Inc); CK Carbon copy, CK Coral and CK Windsong fonts (*Creating Keepsakes*).

Page 86: **Beauty**
Patterned papers and *beauty* icicle letters (KI Memories); letter stickers (Creative Imaginations); Pigma Micron pen (Sakura).

Page 87: **Zeno Family**
Garamouche font (P22 Type Foundry); color-blocked cardstock (Paper Loft); vellum; eyelets; square punch (Marvy Uchida); alphabet rubber stamps (Hero Arts); VersaMark stamping ink (Tsukineko).

Page 87: **The Travels of Ken Champion**
Patterned paper, vellum and tags (Paper Pizazz, Hot Off The Press); star charms (Creative Beginnings); eyelets (Stamp Studio); pen (Gelly Roll, Sakura); gold thread (DMC); CK Cursive and CK Script fonts (*The Best of Creative Lettering,* CD Combo, *Creating Keepsakes*).

Page 87: **Growing by Leaps and Bounds**
Patterned paper (Paper Adventures); Over-alls page topper and border (EK Success); CK Handprint font (*Creating Keepsakes*).

Page 88: **It Is The Sea**
Patterned paper (Karen Foster Design); rivets (Chatterbox, Inc.); Le Plume pens (Marvy Uchida).

Page 89: **Where the Path May Lead**
CK Twilight font (*Creating Keepsakes*); buttons (Hillcreek Designs); foam squares (Therm O Web); quote (Ralph Waldo Emerson).

Page 90: **I Love Bugs**
Renae Lindgren paper; stickers and borders (Creative Imaginations); CK Handprint font (*Creating Keepsakes*).

Page 91: **Friends**
Red metal (Reynolds); Wacky Alphabet template for "d" and "f" (EK Success); silver eyelets, eyelet setting tool and circle Metal

Alphabet "i" (Making Memories); page pebbles (Making Memories); jewelry tag (Avery); Shadow Alphabet rubber stamps "n" (Hero Arts); Nostalgiques Alphabet Sticker "s" (EK Success); red ink; embossing gun (Marvy Uchida); Ultra Thick Embossing Enamel (Suze Weinburg); date stamp (Stockwell); vellum; twine.

Page 91: **FAMILY**
Patterned paper (Colors by Design); ribbon (Offray); walnut ink (Memory Lane); alphabet stamps (PSX); stamp pad (Stampin' Up!); fiber (On the Surface); jute; charm; cardboard; white acrylic paint; tags; black pen; Riverside font (Internet).

Page 93: **A TASTE OF WINTER**
Marydale font (Internet); tag (Avery Dennison); metal snowflakes (Making Memories); snowflake punch (Family Treasures, Inc.); Hannibal Lecter title font (ScrapVillage.com); Butterbrotpapier journaling font (Internet); corrugated paper.

Page 93: **HAPPINESS**
Eyelets (All My Memories); Champagne font (twopeasinabucket.com); daisy punch (Marvy Uchida); ribbon.

Page 94: **PIGGIES**
CK Squiggle font (*Creating Keepsakes*); Kids Letters lettering template (Provo Craft); chalk (Craf-T Products).

Page 95: **SETTING EYELETS**
Eyelet; hole punch; eyelet setter; setting mat and hammer.

Page 96: **MAGNETIC PERSONALITY**
Specialty paper (Magenta); rubber stamps (Stampin' Up!); pen (American Crafts); tags (Avery); fibers (On the Surface); eyelets; mini-brads; mesh (Magneta).

Page 97: **SAND**
Patterned paper (Colorbök); vellum tag; eyelet and Twistel paper yarn (Making Memories); specialty paper (Magenta); pen (American Crafts).

Page 98: **A RANDOM LIST OF THINGS I LOVE**
Ribbed cardstock (Crafter's Workshop); die-cut envelopes (Accu-Cut Systems); square punch (Family Treasures); letter stickers (Colorbök); CK Primary computer font (*The Art of Creative Lettering* CD, *Creating Keepsakes*); tags (DMD Industries); stickers (Mrs. Grossman's, Colorbök, Creative Imaginations; Michel & Co., Paper House); heart punch (Emagination Crafts).

Page 99: **DADDY AND HIS LITTLE GIRL**
Small sand dollars (Magic Scraps); beads (Blue Moon); transparency film (Apollo); photo corners (marthastewart.com); pen (American Crafts); foam core.

Page 100: **MAX J. COULON**
Dark-crackle patterned paper (The Stamping Station); corrugated paper (EK Success); embossed stickers (K & Company); Typist font (Internet); ColorBox stamping ink (Clearsnap, Inc.); hemp; tags (homemade design).

Page 101: **LOVE IS WHAT BINDS US TOGETHER**
Ribbon (Offray); chalk; Cochin Archaic font (Internet).

Page 101: **YOU ARE MY WORLD**
Sonnets patterned paper and Flea Market letter stickers (Creative Imaginations); Pixie Antique letter stamps (PSX Design); Coastal Mesh netting (Magic Scraps); mini brads.

Page 101: **AUTUMN AFTERNOON**
Patterned Paper (Scrap-Ease); vellum (Catscrappin'); Footlight MT Light computer font (Microsoft Word); leaves.

Page 102: **PALS**
Patterned paper (Provo Craft); page topper (Cock-A-Doodle Design, Inc.); CK Journaling font (*Creating Keepsakes*); eyelets (Doodlebug Design); yellow twine (Stampin' Up!).

Page 103: **MCKENNA**
Humanist 521 font (Internet); beads (Suze Weinberg's Tutu Bedazzlers); rose petals; (note: words, beads and rose petals were enclosed in a frame sewed from a page protector using embroidery floss).

Page 103: **TIRE SWING**
Zig writer pen (EK Success); Mary Engelbreit stickers (Creative Imaginations; eyelets (Making Memories); rings (Westrim Crafts).

Page 104: **MY SISTER'S BIRTHDAY**
Patterned paper (Doodlebug Design); pens (Page Doodlers, Cock-A-Doodle Design, Inc; Zig Writers, EK Success); chalks (Craft-T Products).

Page 104: **COOKIE LOVE**
Patterned paper (Paper Fever); vellum (Paper Adventures); Commercial Break computer font (twopeasinabucket.com); stickers (Provo Craft); die cuts (MM's Designs); fibers (Rubba Dub Dub, Art Santcum); brads.

Page 105: **DOORWAYS IN THE STOCKADE**
LD Antique computer font (letteringdelights.com); Garamouche journaling font (P22 Type Foundry); craft wire (Artistic Wire, Ltd.); chalk (Craf-T Products).

Page 105: **BLISS**
Vellum (Bazzill Basics); alphabet rubber stamps (Hero Arts); stamping ink (Stampendous!); Jilted Bride font (twopeasinabucket.com); CK Handprint font (*Creating Keepsakes*); square punch (Family Treasures); circle punch (Marvy Uchida); red and blue eyelets (The Stamp Doctor); yellow and green eyelets (Happy Hammer); Twistel paper yarn (Making Memories).

Page 106: **SMILE!**
Digital page; virtual fibers.

Page 107: **SOCCER IS A KICK!**
HP Creative Scrapbook Assistant; CK Urban and CK Penman font (*Creating Keepsakes*).

Page 108: **ZENKOJI TEMPLE**
Digital camera; textured paper and vellum; brads (HyGlo); Garamond computer font (Microsoft Word).

Page 109: **FOCUS ON WHAT'S AHEAD**
Sony Mavica CD camera; Adobe Photoshop 7.0; Incised 901 BT font (Broderbund PressWriter application).

Page 110: **SMILES ARE THE SOUL'S KISSES**
Digital camera.

Page 111: **SAGUARO**
Digital camera.

Page 113: **MEANT TO BE**
Digital camera.

Page 114: **NEMO**
Adobe Photoshop 7.0; cork paper (Magic Scraps); CK Teacher's Pet font (*Creating Keepsakes*); google eye; vellum; ribbon; beads.

Page 116: **EVOCATIVE**
Burgundy crackle patterned paper (Karen Foster Design); leaf and corn stickers (Jolee's Boutique); chalk.

117: **The Courtship of Philip and Agnes**
Computer-designed patterned papers.

Page 118: **If Roses Grow In Heaven**
Jolee's by You Flower accents (EK Success); Fine Hand title font (Internet); Times New Roman font (Microsoft Word); ribbon; date stamp; ink.

Page 119: **Home, Hearts, and Hands**
Top: Vellum (The Paper Company); CK Cursive computer font (*The Best of Creative Lettering*, CD Vol. 2, *Creating Keepsakes*); eyelets (Impress Rubber Stamps).
Bottom: Vellum (The Paper Company); CK Bella computer font (*The Best of Creative Lettering,* CD Vol. 3, *Creating*

Page 119: **Welcome Home, Baby**
Left: Patterned paper and stickers (All My Memories); CK Tools computer font (*The Best of Creative Lettering,* CD Vol. 2, *Creating Keepsakes*).

Right: Vellum (Paper Adventures); stickers (All My Memories); Bradley Hand ITC computer font (Microsoft Word).

Page 121: **Meeting Face to Face**
Pharmacy title font (AOL); Hootie and Antique Type title and subtitle fonts (Internet); CK Heritage and CK Tea Party journaling fonts (*Creating Keepsakes*); orange beads and square metal-rimmed tag (Shannon Miklo, Scrapbook-Bytes.com).

Pages 122-123: **Airborne**
CK Sketch font (*Creating Keepsakes*).

Page 124: **One Snowy Day**
Vellum (Autum Leaves); buttons (Dress-It-Up, Cut-It-Up).

Page 124: **Sweet Miriam**
Vellum; embroidery floss; tags, letters and eyelets (Making Memories)

Page 125: **Moments**
Think Small and Carpenter computer fonts (twopeasinabucket.com); quote adapted from a Hallmark card.

Pages 126-127: **Celebrating the Everyday Moments**
Vellum; tags, bookplates, CK Gutenberg title font (*Creating Keepsakes*); fonts: Marydale journaling (Internet); Times New Roman (Microsoft Word).

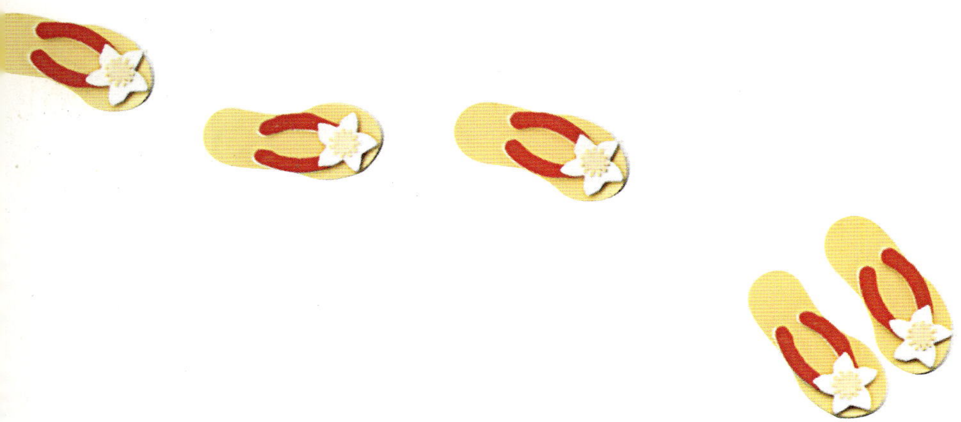